Conquering the Unconquerable

by

J. C. McPheeters

First Fruits Press
Wilmore,
Kentucky
c2018

Conquering the unconquerable by J.C. McPheeters.
First Fruits Press, © 2019
ISBN: 9781621718598 (print), 9781621718604 (digital),
9781621718611(kindle)

Digital version at
http://place.asburyseminary.edu/firstfruitsheritagematerial/161

McPheeters, J. C. (Julian Claudius), 1889-1983.
    Conquering the unconquerable / by J.C. McPheeters. – Wilmore, KY: First
Fruits Press, ©2019.

      143 pages; cm.

      Reprint. Previously published: Louisville, KY: Herald Press, [196-?]
      This book is a collection of messages delivered from the pulpit, over the
      radio, and at the chapel services of Asbury Theological Seminary.
      ISBN: 9781621718598 (pbk.)

      1. Methodist Church--Sermons. 2. Sermons, American.   I. Title.

BX8333.M36 C664 2019

Cover design by Jon Ramsay

asburyseminary.edu
800.2ASBURY
204 North Lexington Avenue
Wilmore, Kentucky 40390

First Fruits
THE ACADEMIC OPEN PRESS OF ASBURY SEMINARY

First Fruits Press
The Academic Open Press of Asbury Theological Seminary
204 N. Lexington Ave., Wilmore, KY 40390
859-858-2236
first.fruits@asburyseminary.edu
asbury.to/firstfruits

CONQUERING

THE UNCONQUERABLE

BY
J. C. McPheeters

HERALD PRESS
LOUISVILLE, KENTUCKY

DEDICATED

To an "elect lady"
My Helpmate
Ethel Chilton McPheeters

PREFACE

This book is a collection of messages delivered from the pulpit, over the radio, and at the chapel services of Asbury Theological Seminary. They are printed practically as they were delivered, except for some alteration in detail.

The purpose of the book is to exalt the victorious Christ, and to attract the reader to the upward look unto Him who will conquer the unconquerable. The defeats and frustrations of life may be turned into victories through Him.

There is always a way of victory where defeat seems inevitable. A mountain-moving faith is not defeated by mountains. We cannot escape the thorns of life, but they may be handled victoriously.

Life's difficulties enhance the great adventure of living. Life moves forward on an ascending scale of triumph, when we continue to march forward with unwavering faith, in the face of every storm. Despair and surrender will thicken the storm clouds, but a victorious faith will outride the storms.

Life's reverses, under the power of a victorious faith, may be transformed into the rounds of a golden ladder which lift the soul to the gateway of heaven. This book closes with some stories of those who have ascended the golden ladder, to stand at the gateway of the City of God.   J. C. M.
Asbury Theological Seminary

CONTENTS

CHAPTER I.

There are multitudes of people all about us who are in a state of utter defeat. Their condition is well illustrated in a story found in the 5th chapter of the Gospel of John which runs as follows:

"Now there is at Jerusalem by the sheep market a pool, which is called in the Hebrew tongue Bethesda, having five porches. In these lay a great multitude of impotent folk, of blind, halt, withered, waiting for the moving of the water. For an angel went down at a certain season into the pool, and troubled the water: whosoever then first after the troubling of the water stepped in was made whole of whatsoever disease he had. And a certain man was there, which had an infirmity thirty and eight years. When Jesus saw him lie, and knew that he had been now a long time in the case, he saith unto him, wilt thou be made whole? The impotent man answered him, Sir, I have no man, when the water is troubled, to put me into the pool: but while I am coming,

5

another steppeth down before me. Jesus saith unto him, Rise, take up thy bed, and walk. And immediately the man was made whole, and took up his bed, and walked."

Here is a picture of a defeated man. For thirty-eight years this man had been lame, during all of which time he found no man to place him in the healing pool. Any attempt that he made to reach the pool was thwarted by others who got there ahead of him. It is evident that the man had yielded and surrendered to his despair. In his defeat. this poor man merely continued to eke out a bare existence. For defeat is a state of mere existence. It offers no vision of the failure. It inspires no efforts to rise above its own dead level. There may be a fatalistic resignation to what is believed to be unconquerable, but there can be no victory.

This man evidently needed some help outside of himself. He did not have the strength within him to rise above his difficulties. Then one day into his wretched life there came the Man of Galilee, the Wonder-Worker of the ages. He who had touched the lives of multitudes transforming sinners into saints, looked with compassion upon this poor, helpless, defeated man. And he, too, was healed of all his diseases.

Jesus is interested in every man who is confronted with defeat. The Man of Galilee, victorious in all phases of His life and never knowing defeat at a single point, is abundantly able not only to deliver us *in* defeat, but also to save us from defeat. He expected it in the case of this man who had been impotent for thirty-eight years. No case of defeat or despair ever in any way baffled Jesus. He was equal to every emergency, to every difficulty, to every problem.

Just as this defeated man found in Jesus new life and power to overcome, so God offers victory to every defeated person. It remains for that person to accept God's offers. The first question that Jesus asked this defeated man was: "Wilt thou be made whole?" The question of Jesus clearly indicates the fact that willingness on the part of the man to be healed was an essential element in his healing. The old proverb,

"Some people enjoy poor health" suggests that there are some people who put forth little or no effort to recover from their chronic ailments. They are reconciled to a state of defeat. They indicate little or no willingness to overcome their difficulties.

Many are in such a state of defeat that they think that any effort on their part to pay the price of victory is futile. This defeated man had surrendered to the idea that he could not be healed, because he had no man to put him in the pool. It had never dawned on him that he might reach the pool in spite of the fact that he had no man to help him. He thus laid the responsibility of his defeat upon another rather than upon himself. Jesus reminded the man that he did not need anybody to put him into the pool, but rather that he should just stand up and walk. It was only when he responded to Christ's command: "Rise, take up thy bed and walk," that the impotent man found healing for his body.

Jesus, the great compassionate friend of mankind, stands ready to help in every difficult situation in life. The question with which He comes to each of us is: "Do you want to be healed? Do you want the burden lifted?" He has given an invitation to men to cast their cares upon Him. The burdens of life are too great for men to try to carry in mere human strength. Men find themselves staggering beneath these burdens, and falling in helpless defeat.

Among the burdens that often bring crushing defeat are those which have their roots in man's natural disposition, a quick temper, for instance. Some people are not willing to be delivered from their evil tempers because their tempers fan their ego. A man with an evil temper may boastfully say: "Nobody can put anything over on me." He may further add: "I told him where to head in." And with these boastful utterances upon his lips he is unwilling to be relieved of his temper. The same may be true concerning a sharp, unkind tongue. There are people who delight in making sharp and unkind remarks about others. The Psalmist David said: "Keep thy tongue from evil and thy lips from speaking guile." The tongue can be a very evil and unruly member of the body. It would seem that some people are so fond of speaking harsh, bitter words that they prefer to indulge their perverted appetite even if it bars them from heaven.

The wise man who wrote the Book of Proverbs says: "He that is slow to anger is better than the mighty; and he that ruleth his spirit than he that taketh a city." The greatest conquest in life is the conquest of ourselves.

Moral and spiritual defeat in the Christian way then is by no means confined to the area of the so-called grosser sins. The parable of the prodigal son tells of two sons in a certain family. Both of these sons were sinners, one in the low sins of the flesh, the other in the high sins of disposition. High sins of disposition may be more respectable, but they are just as sinful as the low sins of the flesh. The son who remained at home was peeved when he saw the royal reception given his wayward brother. Many have ruined their opportunities for success and even fortune by the sin of disposition. The person who is afflicted with this sin often fails to recognize the tragedy of his malady, a condition which makes the sin all the more dangerous. The prodigal who had sunk to the low level of the sins of the flesh readily admitted that he was a sinner. His case was more hopeful than that of the brother who boasted of his good qualities. The swine pen of the prodigal, illustrates one type of sin, and the evil disposition of the brother who remained home illustrates another type. Both of these sins spell wreckage and defeat for the soul, unless they are conquered.

The good news in the gospel message is the fact that both of these sins may be healed. It seems odd that those who may be chained by the bonds of defeat must be persuaded to accept freedom. They remain in their state of defeat in the face of the invitation to liberty. Confronted by a way of release, they turn back to their old prison house of defeat and evil tempers. This is graphically illustrated by an incident in the life of Dwight L. Moody. Some years ago when the great evangelist was speaking before the prisoners of a certain peniten-

tiary, it was announced that at the close of
the service, the Governor would deliver a
pardon to one of the prisoners. When the
pardon was read the man in question, who
was a lifetimer, hesitated for some moments
before he arose to accept the pardon. Not
until some of his cellmates pushed him from
his seat did he go forward. Strange to say,
when the prisoners began the march back
to their cells this man, even though par-
doned, dropped in line to go with them. It
was necessary for attendants to pull him
out saying, "Man, don't you know you're
free?"

Spiritual freedom is a glorious possibility
for every one. It has been made possible
only through the great Liberator of the
souls of men. Jesus Christ came to earth
to set free the captives. During His earthly life He released multitudes bound with
disease, sin, superstition, fear, and the like.
In no case did He ever fail to set the captive free.

What is the liberation you are looking
for in your own life? If it is liberation
from sin, God has promised not only for-

giveness but release from whatever sin may be tormenting you. Through the prophet Isaiah, He said: "Though your sins be as scarlet, they shall be white as snow; though they be red like crimson, they shall be as wool." Are you living in the bondage of some fear? Hear this promise from the Bible: "Perfect love casteth out fear." Perfect trust in God releases the soul from those fears of life which beset us on every hand. Yes, there is victory for us over the fears of life. Do you want release from some evil habit that has fixed itself deep in your life? There is release from that habit, whatever it may be. God is able to break the chains and fetters of every evil habit. The message of Christ to the world is in these words: "He hath sent me to preach deliverance to the captive."

Deliverance is offered to all people alike. It is not conditioned upon race, nationality, education or cultural qualifications. It is conditioned upon our simple faith in accepting the deliverance which He offers. Through this deliverance the impure may become pure, the wicked may become righteous, the burdened and the heavy laden may find rest, the sorrowing may find comfort, the dejected and despairing may find hope. Those sinking in the miry clay may have their feet set upon a solid rock; those having no song may have their hearts set to singing; those who are captive may find deliverance; those who sit in darkness may have a song of cheer for their hearts in the darkest night. The unconquerable may be conquered through the amazing grace of our Lord Jesus Christ.

THE ADVENTURE OF LIVING

CHAPTER II.

Life is a great adventure. Many and varied are the experiences that are possible in the span of a human life. Life holds for us both joys and sorrows. It holds triumphs and defeats. It has its certainties and uncertainties. It is ever in a state of flux, for it never remains the same. Its waters are always changing. It was Heroclitus who said: "You can't bathe twice in the same stream." Life is often a succession of crises. We have hardly passed one crisis until another looms upon the horizon. These crises are usually fraught with great possibilities for man. For while grappling with them, man may be lifted to the heights of happiness or plunged into the depths of despair.

Life is a challenge to the imagination. It is a process in which we are ever planning and dreaming and looking toward the future. If we live successfully we cannot live on the laurels of the past. The successes of yesterday will not suffice for vic-

tories which we are called upon to win today. It is the purpose of God that man
shall meet the challenges which life offers
and thereby keep ascending life's ladder.
Many have never caught the vision of life
in its altitudes. Instead of reaching into
the heights where horizons are widened,
they live in the lowlands. Did not Jesus
announce that the purpose of His coming
into the world was that men might have
this life, and live it abundantly? When life
is thus lived abundantly, we find plenty of
lure and thrill to inspire us zestfully onward.

Life in this higher sphere is creative. In
the Epistle of James, the 1st chapter and
the 22nd verse, is a very practical command:
"Be ye doers of the word, and not hearers
only." This Scripture in substance means:
"Quit listening and do something." Our
actions may speak louder than our words.

One of the hindrances to creative living
is selfishness. Many lives have been
wrecked by becoming self-centered. The
popular mood of today is selfishness. If we
are to live in the highest sphere, we must

cut across this mood. When we cast our bread upon the water for others, it is certain to return to us in the higher blessings of life. Jesus said: "It is more blessed to give than to receive." The life that is ever giving out to others is like the five barley loaves and two small fishes that fed the five thousand. After the five thousand had been fed, they gathered up twelve baskets full of the fragments—and these from an initial five loaves and two fishes. When we are investing our lives for other people in the name of Christ, there is a divine multiplication table that is ever in operation for the increase of our spiritual assets.

Another attitude that frustrates creative living is that which is satisfied with merely maintaining the *status quo*. Such an attitude lives upon the same dead level from day to day. Life to be triumphant and victorious must move upon an ascending scale. We should never be satisfied with the achievements of the past. The moment we begin to rest upon what we have already accomplished, we begin a retreat. Past experiences will bring to us many things of value for our guidance in the future. But these should be used only as stepping stones to the higher heights of living. Mere loyalty to the good things of the past may spell stagnation. It is not uncommon to find a sound orthodoxy afflicted with dry rot. When life is lived on an ascending scale, it is a constantly expanding adventure.

Christianity continues to attract and hold its grip upon the people because Christianity is life and life is always growth. Jesus came into the world, not to establish a religion, but to reveal to men *the* way of life. He said: "I am the way, the truth, and the life." Jesus was never concerned that His disciples merely observe a set of rules; He *was* concerned that they follow Him. In so doing, the rules would not only be kept; they would be the basis of growth, of that continuing, ever-expanding adventure of life in God.

When we live our lives on this ascending scale, new situations constantly confront us. Every victory in life precipitates a new situation with some new testing, some new problems to be solved. Strange new choices are constantly being thrust upon us. These choices are to be made, not on the basis of human strength and wisdom, but in response to God's divine guidance. For there is a divine guidance for men in this world of perplexity, problem, and sorrow. By ourselves, we know not the way we should go. We may intend to go the right way, and then choose the wrong way. Our response to divine guidance makes life a partnership with God. With Him as senior partner in the firm, we can never become spiritually bankrupt.

Many people are standing idly by waiting for some dream, some utopia, some great opportunity to come their way before they set their hands to immediate tasks. Such individuals are described in Matthew, chapter 20, verses 6 and 7. There the question is asked, "Why stand ye here all the day idle? They say unto him, because no man has hired us." This Scripture describes little groups of men standing idly by in the market place at Nazareth toward the close of the day. Those who have stood idly around in their delay to begin living life in the higher sphere have not as yet learned the real significance of life.

One of the secrets of living is the realization that life cannot be lived in its fullest without dependence upon God. When men have assumed the attitude that they themselves are the proprietors of their own lives, they are living in a state of illusion. The fact that men today are attempting to run their lives independent of God, is eloquent testimony to the perversion of human nature. Life becomes unmanageable when lived on the lower material plane, without recognition of God. Jesus likened life to a vineyard of which He was the Master and Proprietor.

We should not be mislead by the popular viewpoint that the highest living depends upon outward conditions and circumstances. Favorable living conditions are certainly to be sought after, but they do not comprise the final word for the highest living. It is quite important that every man have a living wage, and not only a living wage, but also a saving wage. We should insist that every man have a proper share in the world's comforts. This is important, but it is not the chief end of man. Jesus did not describe as happy those folks who possessed *things*. He did not say in the Sermon on the Mount: "Blessed are the people who have a living wage. Blessed are they who are at leisure, and have their share of comfort." It is evident that Jesus wanted people to enjoy these temporal blessings, but He was vastly more concerned about spiritual values. The Sermon on the Mount deals with these when it says, "Blessed are the peacemakers, for they shall be called the children of God."

Life in the higher sphere is a life of work. A few years ago people thought that they could ride the stock market into the clover of prosperity, but they were disappointed. More recently men have thought that they could bring in the millennium with shorter working hours, higher wages, and more leisure time. While these things are important, they cannot meet man's greatest need, which is spiritual.

God's plan for happiness and success is not measured in higher wages, shorter hours, more leisure time, or in financial independence. These things have not brought to life the deeper and more abiding happiness. Humanity has ever been embarking upon life's pilgrimage with these false goals of happiness, and as a result life has been littered with failures. According to God's standards, it is not the high-powered "go-getters" that are called successful. Happiness is the result of a certain kind of life built upon a certain kind of faith—faith in the all-conquering Christ as the remedy for every human need.

This philosophy of God concerning happiness is queer to the world, but the philosophy that has brought to the world so much frustration in this modern age is still stranger. The life that God offers through Christ is not dependent for its happiness upon outward conditions or circumstances. Such a life is invested with a key that unlocks closed doors, and marches on to triumph and victory in the face of all the besetting obstacles that may be met along the journey.

THE VICTORIOUS LIFE

CHAPTER III.

The word "victorious" is always rich in meaning, but never more so than when coupled with the word "life." The quest for the victorious life is universal. In all areas of human endeavor people are in quest of victory. This has often been powerfully demonstrated by men and women in pursuit of the material values of life. "Success" and "victory," however, are watchwords not of these alone, but of the human race generally. The world has always sought to identify itself with the winning side, reserving its laurels for the victor, and its thorns for the vanquished. The contagious character of success is clearly demonstrated when a fickle public turns to the winning side, too often at the sacrifice of principle. The cumulative effect of success is apparent in the spiritual life; for the Scriptures describe just this in the phrase "from glory to glory." It can be no violation of Scripture to express it thus, "from victory to victory."

Indeed, victory is always cumulative at compound interest. Each victory won paves the way for other victories. But defeat seems even more contagious; it carries us down as rapidly as a toboggan on the mountain snow. If it be whispered that a man's business is slipping, loss of patronage, always results. Instead of that man's friends rallying around him at such a time, they will forsake him, like people leave a sinking ship.

The quest for victory among nations comprises a large part of the world's history. Such quests for victory are often charged with disappointment. Nations have arisen to world power only to crumble into obscurity. Men of personality and ambition have made their appearance on the world's stage. For a brief day they shone like stars in the firmament. Suddenly the curtain dropped, covering them with obscurity. The victories of Alexander and Napoleon were not enduring. For a little while they shot like flaming comets across the horizon, only to vanish forever from sight. These quests for the emoluments of earth are constantly going on in this restless world. Their fruition is like the bubble which may be punctured with a pin prick. The eternal quest for victory in the material things of life meets with defeat which is as universal as the quest itself. Thus there seems to be an irony of fate which mocks us continually.

There is one important thing which we overlook in our quest for victory in material things. Whether we know it or not, in our pursuit we are really seeking for something more than they have to offer. We thought we wanted wealth, fame, honor, but in truth we wanted something over and beyond these things. Whatever worldly goals a man reaches there still remains the restless urge in his heart for something more. The end of every man's quest is that victory for which his heart craves, the victory of the eternal Spirit, which outlives all that is earthly. Mere things can never satisfy, for man himself is something more than a thing. *Things* are temporal and fleeting. Man is enduring, living unto all eternity.

The building of a temporal kingdom, enduring only for a day, can never satisfy him who is to live for ever. The only kingdom that is enduring is the Kingdom of God.

This kingdom knows no defeat. It outlives principalities and powers, and even worlds. Man's only hope of victory is to be identified with this kingdom, which is eternal.

The New Testament reveals that the door into this kingdom is Jesus Christ. He is spoken of by one of the prophets as, "The desire of all nations." This description of Him expresses the universal heart cry of men for Christ. He is the desire of all nations, the object of the universal quest of man, because He alone can bring universal victory. He brings victory over sin, for He who endured every temptation known to man, was himself without sin. He brings victory over deep-seated national hatreds and prejudices, for He is the universal Friend of all men. In Him, moreover, is found victory over death, for He conquered the grave. Jesus is the only one who has conquered death, and through Him men have been able to say: "Oh, death, where is thy sting; O grave, where is thy victory?"

The nations have ignored the Prince of Peace. The many plans for peace which

have been adopted have ignored the one and
only plan by which peace can come: the
realization of u n i v e r s a l brotherhood
through the Prince of Peace.

When Jesus said, "I am the way, the
truth, and the life," He gave to the world
the only dependable solution of economic
and racial problems, and the only dependable and enduring platform for world peace.
So long as men reject the Prince of Peace,
wars will be fought, empires will rise and
fall, and civilization will continue to experience its "dark ages."

The early Christians attracted the attention of the world because of their triumphant victories over enemies both from
within and without. The secret of victory
in their lives is to be attributed to their
wholehearted devotion and unreserved consecration to Christ, their Lord and Saviour.
They went forth into a wicked and sinful
world, completely consecrated men and
women. And all because they had exper-
ienced in their hearts the sanctifying grace
of Christ. For Pentecost brought to the
followers of Christ a victory which they had
never witnessed before.

In His valedictory prayer at the Last Supper, Jesus prayed for His disciples in these words: "Sanctify them through thy truth; thy word is truth. . . . and for their sake I sanctify myself that they also might be sanctified through the truth." In this prayer Jesus prayed for a consecrated, sanctified, Spirit-filled, Spirit-led church. This prayer shows us the way to victory.

Before Jesus ascended into heaven, He commanded His disciples to tarry at Jerusalem until they be endued with power from on high. It was in response to this command that the disciples laid aside everything, and gave attention to the one thing needed: tarrying in the upper room until the coming of the Holy Spirit in His cleansing and enduing power. On that day victory was inscribed upon the banners of those hundred and twenty souls. No power in earth or hell could defeat them. That victory is for the church of God today. It is for every soul who will pay the price of the completely consecrated life, crowned with a step of faith in Christ's sanctifying power. The victory is worth the price. If we pay the price, we shall obtain the victory, and eventually we shall wear the crown.

MODERN DILEMMAS OF LIFE

CHAPTER IV.

This complex age presents to modern man many a dilemma. In many respects, life in our highly mechanized age is quite different to that found in the argicultural civilization of the past. The fundamental moral and spiritual needs of man, however, are the same in every age.

The great spiritual realities grasped by men in the more simple periods of the race's development abide until this day. Common to men in all ages are certain physical needs such as light, air, and water. Certain spiritual realities are essential to the needs of the inner man even as certain physical elements are essential to needs of outer man. Fundamental spiritual realities are faith, hope, and love. These are abiding and enduring, and men will need them as long as the earth stands.

One of the stumbling blocks in every age has been the temptation for man to trust himself. One of the most important things

29

for us to discover in life is that we in our human strength alone are not equal to life's burdens and responsibilities. The ancient Greeks and Romans erred in this particular in thinking that they were sufficient in themselves. They built up a civilization on the conception that man is able to supply his own needs and fight his own battles. The Greeks majored in the cultivation of the mind. The Golden Age of Greek philosophy and culture is still looked upon as a remarkable period in history. It is true that Greece for a time prospered, but the sequel to Greek supremacy does not make pleasant reading. Rome came later, with her ambitious program for the redemption of human life by law and order. Both the Romans and the Greeks tried to deal with humanity upon the human level, and their attempt proved a failure.

In the 18th century, under the leadership of men like Rousseau, France made another attempt after the order of the ancient Greeks and Romans. This effort of humanity to build on its own level again proved futile. As a commentary on France's perversion, we find Rosseau weeping at the death of his dog but sending without a a tremor his five illegitimate children to a foundling asylum. When humanity tries to build on itself it builds upon unstable emotions, fickle intellects, and confused morals.

The lasting honors of life belong only to those who look forward and upward. When men look backward and downward, and begin to build upon humanity's own level, they can never hope to experience happiness that comes only to those that have the upward look. In relying on his strength man falls below the standard of a common order of decency and success to a level that is brutish rather than human. Man's trust in himself then constitutes a major dilemma of modern life.

Another dilemma of modern man is concerned with his finding the right and proper balance in his perspective of such realities as life, eternity, and the business of living in the present world. There is a faith that tries to spend all of its working hours in heaven, leaving very little time for earth.

Its practitioners escape the practical, every day problems of life by meditating upon the life that is to come. They take the position that this life matters but little, that they can afford to let it go by without much serious attention.

It is quite proper that some thought and attention be given to the after life, but we must not overlook the fact that as human beings we live amid the realities of this world, that a victorious faith must come to grips with the every day affairs of life. We still live in a world where people get sick, where they die, where wars are fought, where panics come, where nations rise and fall, where civilizations come and go in the shifting scenes of the drama of the ages.

Over against this kind of faith, with its misplaced emphasis on the after life, we have had a reaction that has reversed things even to the point of violence. So instead of giving attention to the things of the after life, we have centered our effort entirely on the things of earth. Some one has expressed this trend thus: "We have thrown out the baby with the bath."

We have developed a materialism that gives little thought or attention to immortality. Many have dismissed the idea of immortality with a wave of the hand, saying: "It is too much for us." While modern life is filled with feverish activities, many have discovered its futility. In the emptiness of our devotion and consecration to the mere things of earth, there are many who have come to say: "We aren't even sure that life is worth while."

Today there are ten thousand forces trying to convince us that man is something less than soul. Men are being ordered about collectively in platoons. Totalitarian governments endeavor to convince men that they are only the minions of something called nationalism. A certain type of science in our time has defined life as a breaking out of the skin of a measly planet. The science that teaches that life came only by an accidental collocation of atoms refuses to accept any moral responsibility for the use which men make of their scientific discoveries. This new science teaches that man is only an automaton directed by irresistible forces over which he has no control. We have forgotten that in this world of fixedness there is a certain variability, that there is a law of contingency in a world of so-called fixed laws. There is a place in such a world for man's free will which, aided by God may make man master of a glorious destiny.

Another dilemma which modern man confronts is that of the appalling odds that are against him in so many of his endeavors. Human strength has proved to be insufficient against them. The burden of things has come to rest heavily upon human shoulders. Millions are being crushed today by these materialistic burdens. These overwhelming, opposing odds catch many men off their guard, and in yielding to the temptation that confronts them, men become less than men.

Men are offering their daily sacrifices today on the altar of business, science, and the state. The totalitarian state presents a new modern god for worship. The worship of this god was a contributing factor in plunging the whole world into the most terrible wars of history. Worship at these altars renews no man's courage, beyond teaching him to whistle in the dark. It is bitter for man to be less than himself, but this is exactly what he becomes when he worships at the altars of these gods.

It is into this world with its broken, disappointed souls, that there comes the voice of one echoing o'er all the wrecks of time: "Come unto me all ye that labor and are heavy laden, and I will give you rest." There is a fair haven with an anchorage in this world of storms. There is a resting place for the souls of men. That resting place may be found in the one whom the Psalmist discovered in the long ago when he said: "The Lord is my refuge and strength, a very present help in trouble." Life's dilemmas may be cleared away, and the soul may rise in triumph and victory in a conquering faith. There is a way of ruin and defeat. There is a way of triumph and victory. It is the way of the upward look which leads men ever onward, forward, to the land of new conquests, new triumphs, and unending victories.

HIDDEN STREAMS FOR LIFE'S MALADIES

CHAPTER V.

Life's victories spring from the hidden streams, those inner waters that replenish the soul and that are invisible to the world. The greatest example of a life nourished and sustained by these hidden streams is that of the Man of Galilee. Well might He say to His disciples: "I have meat to eat that ye know not of." He counselled the woman at the well: "Whosoever drinketh of the water that I shall give him shall never thirst." He spoke quietly of streams of water flowing out of the heart. To find the secret of His life, one must look for these hidden streams whence He drew His inspiration and His power. It was during those times of quiet retreat, away from the busy murmur of the world, that He tapped this hidden fountain of living waters.

A grape vine in England, more than two hundred years old, and long famed for its fruitage, was once the pride of kings and princes. In process of time it ceased to bear fruit. The gardener was instructed to put forth every effort to make the historic vine produce again. All his efforts failed. Some years later, to the astonishment of the gardener, the vine again began to bear its usual fruit. Investigating, the gardener dug deep down into the ground about the roots of the vine, down many feet through the dry dirt until he discovered that the roots touched the waters of the Thames River far beneath the surface of the earth. For some reason, best known to nature, the vine had been cut off from her source of supply. It was fresh contact with the hidden stream below that caused the historic vine to bear fruit again. So often it is in life that people become discouraged; they no longer bring forth the fruit of achievement as in former days. They are tempted to despair. The maladies of life beset them on the right hand and on the left. They lose the hidden stream from which new sources of power may ever be drawn.

This hidden stream whence we may draw strength against the maladies of life gives us the will to go on in the face of difficulties and obstacles. Some years ago some one sent me a card bearing this significant paragraph:

"It is the unanimous testimony of great souls that their best discoveries have come just after they thought that they would have to give up, because they could not go on; but who, in dogged determination, kept pushing beyond what seemed to them to be the limit of their endurance."

It is an old proverb: "The darkest hour is just before the dawn." The men who have succeeded in life have had the will to go on at the point where others have stopped. In hard circumstances we are constantly tempted to quit and look back upon easier times. We need ever bear in mind the fate of Lot's wife who, in the backward look, turned to a pillar of salt. The way of victory and triumph is in the forward, upward look.

Another need that this hidden stream supplies against the evil day is the grace of a forgiving spirit. Much of failure in the Christian life is due to bitterness and resentment taking up their abode within the soul. This bitterness usually expresses itself through a cynical spirit and an unforgiving attitude. The providences of life which have hemmed us in with handicaps come in for much abuse. But men will never find relief in an unforgiving attitude toward the providence that permitted a wall to hem them in. Such walls may be scaled only by those whose hearts are free from the rancor of unforgiveness. As Archer Wallace says: "Our greatest victories are spiritual conquests and no man has been defeated who has conquered hate."

The battle to rise above the handicaps of life is severe enough without adding to its fierceness the additional burden of an unforgiving spirit. A truly great soul possesses a forgiving spirit. Henry Ward Beecher manifested such a spirit of forgiveness toward all who treated him ill until it became a proverb in Brooklyn: "If you want a favor from Beecher, kick him." Resentment is poison for the soul, and no life can live in triumph and victory with the smouldering fires of resentment hidden within.

People often cherish their hatreds and resentments after the manner of the natives of Polynesia. They spend most of their time fighting. It is customary for these natives to keep some reminder of their hatreds ever before them. They have certain articles suspended from the roof of their huts to keep alive the memory of the wrongs inflicted upon them. Lest their hatreds and resentments might vanish with the passing of time, they keep before them bones and other objects to fan the flame of resentment.

God expects us to forgive and to forget. Is not our own forgiveness by God conditional upon our forgiveness of others? Jesus said: "For if ye forgive not men their trespasses, neither will your Father in heaven forgive your trespasses."

And how shall a man discover God's hidden streams, except through prayer? God is sufficient for every human need, whatever it may be. God knocks at the door of every heart, seeking to come in, to meet every need. Prayer is the method which God ordained to release His power for the needs of men. It is the means by which we open the door to let God in to meet our needs. It is the mightiest force available to men. It is prayer that makes the difference in the way things go in our lives.

It was through prayer that George Washington found hidden strength during the discouraging winter at Valley Forge. It was the dawning of a new day for Saul of Tarsus when these words were spoken of him, "Behold, he prayeth." They transformed the life of Saul, that his name was changed from Saul to Paul.

Life's bitter experiences may be sweetened by prayer. The impassable chasm across our pathway may be spanned by prayer. Towering mountains that confront us may be lifted through prayer. Lowering clouds with their darkening shadows may be rent asunder through prayer. Not without reason did Jesus say: "Men ought always to pray and not to faint."

When you go from your knees to any task you will be more efficient in meeting that task. Prayer yields the greatest dividend of any investment, and yet it seems that only a comparatively few people avail themselves of the investment. Did you neglect to pray today? Then if you neglected to pray, you lost something of great value in your life. Take time to pray every day, and your life will be nourished by hidden streams that will help you meet every need of your life.

It is not the will of our heavenly Father that any should ever surrender to discouragement, but that all should avail themselves of the strength which prayer alone can bring. Remember again: "Men ought always to pray, and not to faint."

UNAFRAID OF LIFE'S TERRORS

CHAPTER VI.

"He that dwelleth in the secret place of the most high shall abide under the shadow of the Almighty. I will say of the Lord, he is my refuge and my fortress: my God; in him will I trust. Surely he shall deliver thee from the snare of the fowler, and from the noisome pestilence. He shall cover thee with his feathers, and under his wings shalt thou trust: his truth shall be thy shield and buckler. Thou shalt not be afraid for the terror by night; nor for the arrow that flieth by day; nor for the pestilence that walketh in darkness; nor for the destruction that wasteth at noonday. A thousand shall fall at thy side, and ten thousand at thy right hand, but it shall not come nigh thee. Only with thine eyes shalt thou behold and see the reward of the wicked. Because thou hast made the Lord, which is my refuge, even the most high thy, habitation; there shall no evil befall thee, neither shall any plague come nigh thy dwelling. For he shall give his angels charge over thee, to keep thee in all thy ways. They shall bear thee up in their hands, lest thou dash thy foot against a stone. Thou shalt tread upon the lion and adder: the young lion and the dragon shalt thou trample under feet. Because he hath set his love upon me, therefore will I deliver him: I will set him on high, because he hath known my name. He shall call upon me, and I will answer him: I will be with him, and honor him. With long life will I satisfy him, and show him my salvation." (Psalm 91).

This is one of the most beautiful of all the Psalms. Although Hebrew scholars tell us that no modern language portrays its beauty, even its English translation holds us in rapt attention every time we read it.

In the first verse is the promise of divine protection: "He that dwelleth in the secret place of the most high shall abide under the shadow of the almighty." Two words attract in this verse: "dwelleth" and "secret place." There are different planes of living, ranging from the low plane of the prodigal in a pen feeding swine herd, to the high plane of Peter, James, and John in the presence of their Lord on the Mount of

Transfiguration.

On what plane are you living? If on the plane of communion and fellowship with our infinite and loving heavenly Father, then you have discovered the golden secret of life. This secret is worth more than all the wealth of Croesus, and all the riches of a Rockefeller. Blessed indeed is that soul whose life is centered in the secret place of the Most High. Jesus could say: "I have meat to eat that ye know not of." In the secret place of the Most High we find hidden resources of strength.

In the Ozark hills of Missouri and Arkansas are the greatest springs to be found anywhere on the American continent. I have visited most of these large springs in this Ozark country, and have stood in wonder at the inexhaustible supply of fresh, living water, ever gushing forth from hidden places in the earth. These springs are fountains of life. The sources of their supply are hidden, and yet they are never exhausted. The volume of supply of many of these springs never varies, even in the midst of famine and drought. Men, too, may find a hidden source of supply, strength, and encouragement. That supply is all the more real because it is neither visible to the naked eye nor tangible to human touch. This hidden source which the Psalmist refers to in the first verse of this 91st Psalm is the "secret place of the Most High."

"I will say of the Lord, he is my refuge and my fortress." In the pioneer days of this country, forts were built for the refuge of the people against Indian uprisings. Into these forts people fled for safety when danger was imminent. Whole neighborhoods would gather in a single fort for protection. These forts, it should be remembered, protected only against those dangers which threatened their bodies. There are greater dangers in life than those that threatened the body. For these that imperil the soul jeopardize our eternal welfare. And how imminent are they! In the face of them it is imperative to remember that we have a fortress and a protection against them: "I will say of the Lord, *he* is my refuge and my fortress."

The third verse reads in part: "Surely

he shall deliver thee from the snare of the fowler." The hunter that goes forth in quest of wild fowl may use a lure to deceive the birds. The common lure is the decoy, which entices the birds bringing them in reach of the hunter's gun. So Satan uses many traps and snares to deceive men. From such the Lord has promised to deliver His people.

"He shall cover thee with his feathers, and under his wings shalt thou trust." So reads the fourth verse, reminding us of Christ's lament over Jerusalem: "O Jerusalem, Jerusalem, how oft would I have gathered you unto myself as a hen gathereth her brood, and ye would not." The hen with her brood is a simple and homely illustration, but it portrays the protecting care of our heavenly Father. The hen is ever on guard as her brood hovers about her. At the first sign of danger, she is quick to sound the warning note which brings her little ones fleeing to her for protection. She hovers over her young at night, protecting them from the cold with her warmth. From the dawning of the day till the settling of the dusk she never relaxes either in the quest of food for her brood, or in her protection over them. Infinitely more, our heavenly Father offers His love and protection to His children. "He shall cover thee with his feathers, and under his wing shalt thou trust."

The latter part of this same verse reads: "His truth shall be thy shield and buckler." This generation stands deeply in need of the truth of God, the deepest of all human needs. It is a shield sufficient to turn away the fiercest darts and arrows We seem to be in a mad rush for everything but the truth as it is in Christ. God's truth is sobering. It knows no respector of persons. It strikes at the roots of sin wherever it may be found. It is a comfort to those who accept it, and it is a judgment upon those who reject it.

The fifth verse begins: "Thou shalt not be afraid." Then the Psalmist enumerates the things which the children of God shall not fear. Among them are "the terror by night" and "the destruction that wasteth at noon day." Today fear hangs like a cloud over many souls. Many a man could say with Thomas Hobbs, the noted philosopher, "Fear and I are twins." Let us rejoice and thank God that the sting of life's fears may be removed. Jesus said: "Let not your heart be troubled, neither let it be afraid." Repeatedly He exhorted His disciples to confidence instead of fear. He said: "Fear not, little flock," and again: "Lo, I am with you always, even unto the end of the world." When I was a small child I was afraid to go into a dark room alone, but I was not afraid when my father walked by my side holding my hand. Neither should we be afraid, even though we may be called to walk through darkness, or taste of bitter waters. Our heavenly Father will hold our hand.

The words of verse 11 are: "For he shall give his angels charge over thee to keep thee in all thy ways." Here we have some light on the office of angels. and perhaps some intimation of the way in which we may be employed in heaven. The angels have definite tasks delegated to them by the heavenly Father. They help guard and protect

His children in this world. The New Testament version runs: "And he shall give his angels charge over thee, and in their hands they shall bear thee up, lest thou dash thy foot against a stone." (Matthew 4:6). The angels are charged to keep us in all our ways. Many times along life's way we have been restrained from pursuing some course which would have meant our wreckage and ruin. We have been made to marvel at our escape from many threatened dangers. May not the secret of our deliverance be found in the fact that the angels of God kept us? In yet another place the Psalmist says: "The angel of the Lord encampeth round about them that fear him." (Psalm 34:7).

In the 14th verse of the Psalms, under consideration we have the promise: "I will be with him in trouble." God does not promise to keep us from *having* trouble; He does promise to be with us *in* trouble. The Psalm closes with the words: "With long life will I satisfy him, and show him my salvation." Let us thank God for His protection along the journey of life. He has promised to go with us all the way, never to leave us nor forsake us.   When our lives are anchored in God's will, we have the assurance of His protecting care, until our work in this earthly pilgrimage is finished.   Whether this pilgrimage be long or short as men evaluate years, the life with which God will satisfy His children is eternal.

THE THORN OF LIFE

One of the misinterpretations of faith has been that it guarantees deliverance from the thorn of life. Jesus never promised His disciples that they would escape "dungeon, fire, and sword." On the other hand, He warned them in advance that these things would come upon them: "Men will hate you and persecute you, and drive you from city to city, and kill you, thinking they do God's service. . . But he that endureth to the end shall be saved."

The victory of faith which overcomes the world, according to the Scriptures, is not the victory of escape from calamity for yourself or your dear ones. It is not uncommon to meet people who have become cynical and skeptical because they prayed for deliverance from some calamity, and deliverance did not come. Some of them say: "I no longer believe in God." But religion is not a magic cloak which we may throw about ourselves and our loved ones, and thereby escape all suffering and disappointment. If religion could be used as such, men would adopt it, not of love for God, but rather as an insurance policy, in which religion would lose its nature, and faith would lose its character. After all, the symbol of Christianity is the cross, not the horseshoe.

The Apostle Paul had a physical affliction which he called his thorn in the flesh. He prayed very earnestly for the removal of this thorn, but it was not taken away. He did receive, however, definite answer in the words: "My grace is sufficient for thee." The victory of faith for Paul was not the removal of his physical affliction, but rather his appropriation through faith of the infinite resources of God that sustained and gave him victory in the midst of his physical affliction.

The victory of faith does not deliver us from the risks of life. The man of faith must take the risks in life that others take. In travel, in war, in sickness, he faces the same possibilities of calamity that others face. Men who have a strong and abiding faith in God are in automobile accidents every day. They are stricken with diseases every day. They are confronted with the same dangers on battlefields as the men who make no profession of faith. But some will say: "If, then, the man of faith encounters the same risks of accidents, disease, and calamities in war, what is the advantage of such a faith?" A victory of mere escape from physical affliction is no victory at all. But the victory that transcends the thorn of life is a real victory.

While God has not promised that we shall escape the bitter waters, He has promised to be with us when we pass through them. The righteous must pass through the valley of the shadow of death just the same as the wicked, but the righteous have this promise: "Yea, though I walk through the valley of the shadow of death, I will fear no evil; for thou art with me, thy rod and thy staff they comfort me."

The victories of faith, then, are not to be measured in the same terms in which the world evaluates success. God is able to turn temporary defeat into final victory through channels of faith. Faith can turn the low tides of defeat into high tides of victory.

God is able to do more with a defeated, penitent nation than with a proud, victorious nation, relying upon her own strength instead of humbly trusting God. Such a proud nation, without trust in God, may continue to pursue successfully a course of paganism, materialism, and international sophistry. According to the record, her moral and spiritual salvation is likely to be found *only* when the tide turns against her. Defeat at times proves a healthy spiritual condition for both men and nations. When all other foundations have been swept away, men may then turn to God.

The things which we long and pray for do not always contribute to our highest good. One of the greatest lessons of faith is that those things which we call calamities and disasters may contribute even more than do those things for which we are continually praying, as for example success, health, and deliverance from bereavement, suffering, and poverty. The Apostle Paul had learned this lesson of faith to a degree that enabled him to say: "I have learned in whatsoever state I am, therewith to be content. I know both how to be abased, and I know how to abound; everywhere and in all things I am instructed both to be full and to be hungry, both to abound and to suffer need. I can do all things through Christ which strengtheneth me."

We are not to understand that a victorious faith extends a welcome to evil. Every legitimate means should be used to ward off evil of every kind. Paul did not yield to the physical affliction of a thorn in the flesh without a heroic struggle for its removal. He prayed earnestly three times for its removal, and no doubt tried every natural means of cure known to his day. But after he had tried every honorable means of escape, he received the guarantee of the sufficiency of God's grace, not only to sustain him in his affliction, but also to give him complete victory over it. Instead of having the thorn removed Paul received strength to handle the thorn. This was a greater victory than mere removal of the trouble. It is a greater victory to triumph in the presence of the thorn than to triumph in its absence.

Since we are surrounded by the widely-spread destructive fires of the world, there remains only one channel for victory—the channel of faith. Through faith in God these furnaces of destruction may be turned into fires of purification. Job speaks of the furnace which refines the gold when he says: "When he hath tried me, I shall come forth as gold." The Psalmist also made reference to the refining fires of the furnace: "For thou, O God, hast proved us: thou hast tried us, as silver is tried." He adds a further observation on the refining fires of the furnace: "We went through fire and through water: but thou broughtest us out into a wealthy place."

The evil fires in the world have not been lighted by God. These fires do not represent His will. But when they are lighted by evil men, God's power is such that He may utilize the evil for blessing upon those whose faith is anchored in Him. If God permits His children to pass through the fire, He will be found in the fire with them also.

Faith in God does not disassociate us from

the heartbreaking sorrows around us. Mary, Martha, and Lazarus were intimate friends of Jesus, but death struck in that home just as it did in other homes. There was a difference, however, in the home of Mary and Martha when death struck claiming their brother. It was the friendship of Jesus that made the difference. In this particular instance Jesus removed the thorn by raising Lazarus from the dead. Such is not always the method of the Master. It only proved His ability to cope with any situation, however difficult it might be.

With many others of His disciples, Jesus does not remove the thorn; instead He gives grace and strength to meet the need. It was more important for the sorrowing Mary and Martha that they had Christ with them than that He should raise their brother from the dead. Had He seen fit not to raise Lazarus, the sisters, in the comfort of His immediate presence, could still have victory.

There is a difference between Christian faith and pagan optimism. Pagan optimism may be boastful, self-sufficient, and proud. Pagan optimism may know all the psychological tricks of mental "pump priming" for producing a sense of confidence and self-sufficiency, but Christian faith wins its victories upon an entirely different basis. It achieves its greatest victories when man is ready to acknowledge that he cannot alone reach his goal. The world arrived at its phesent state of chaos and confusion through the self-sufficient efforts of men who in their boastful pride have left God out of their plans.

For its victories, Christian faith is not sustained by the dream of some man-made utopia. Its motivation is that long-promised, divinely-inspired kingdom of "Peace on earth, good will toward men." Although the path that leads thither is strewn with thorns, it is a path of glorious victory. The victory of the early church was in an unfriendly world. Through faith the early disciples were more than conquerors over principalities, powers, and spiritual wickedness in high places. Victories obtained in the catacombs, at the martyr's stake, and in the lion's den are still available in a confused, sophisticated, modern world. "This is the victory that overcomes the world, even our faith."

LIVING VICTORIOUSLY WITH PEOPLE

CHAPTER VIII.

The Bible says: "No man liveth unto himself, and no man dieth unto himself." This statement is literally true. It is impossible to live a life alone without some kind of contact with other people. The problem of living with other people is one of the biggest problems of life. Those who have found the secret to this problem have scaled one of the highest hurdles in the race of life. The world has been periodically cursed with war because men have failed to find the secret of living together successfully.

The manager of a leading hotel in one of America's largest cities says: "I have to fire more people because they can't get along with their associates or their superiors than for any other reason. Seventy-five per cent of our dismissals are for this reason." People are constantly failing because of their human relationships. They fail in business, they fail in the home, they fail in living victoriously in their personal lives.

In this matter of getting along with people we must recognize certain difficulties. We are sure, for instance, to meet people whom we do not like. Certain personalities will irritate us. Some will "get on our nerves." But it is to be remembered that while I contact individuals whose personalities irritate me, my own make-up may irritate some one else. If we are to get along with people we must be interested in people, in their likes and dislikes. One sure way *not* to get along with people is to be self-centered oneself. The burden of the conversation of some people always centers about themselves. That person who can focus the conversation upon the interests of the other person has taken one of the biggest steps toward friendship. Incidentally, we should ever bear in mind that we can always learn something from every person.

Self control is an indispensable factor in getting along with other people. In fact, the bigger the man the greater his self control. You can measure a man rather well by those things which he allows to throw his temper out of balance. Men without temper are weaklings; for it is temper that gives strength for the battle of life. But temper must be controlled if we are going to get along with people. Instead of controlling their tempers, many are controlled *by* them. Such are the victims of a slavery that grows more oppressive with the passing of the years. The free man is he who has learned to accept the jars of life without showing irritation, without losing control. Indeed, he is held a weakling who has lost control of temper, appetite, or any other normal desire of life.

Herein is one of the great secrets of the life of Jesus. No one ever saw Him lose His self-control. He was calm and considerate in all of life's emergencies. Not even in His most devastating denunciations can one find evidence of His having lost His normal poise. He who was master of the storm at sea was also master of Himself.

To get along with other people, moreover, we must be reconciled to criticism. No man has ever lived who has been able to avoid criticism. The best and greatest Character

that earth ever knew was crucified upon a
cross.   If we accept criticisms in the right
spirit, making them creative, we may use
them as stepping stones for improvement.

Dr. George R. Stuart was one of the
greatest preachers the southland ever had.
He was the traveling companion of the celebrated Sam P. Jones for sixteen years.
Later in life he occupied the largest
churches of his denomination. When George
Stuart started out as a young preacher he
made it a rule to have a certain person in
his congregation criticize him; in fact, he
said, this experience was so helpful that he
would not be without such criticism even
if it meant his making some financial sacrifice.   In those days when he was a platform speaker of national reputation, he re-
ferred repeatedly to that early criticism as
among the most helpful experiences of his
life.

We should train ourselves not to be upset by criticism, but rather seeking to weigh
carefully all the criticism that comes to us.
The man who has as an enemy criticized
you, may prove to be your best friend by

the insights he gives you. On the other hand we too must guard against a kind of critical approach, all too common, that goes something like this: "I would not harm Mr. John Doe for all the world. I really have been his friend, but—did you hear this or that?" This techinque in which we append a "but" clause to our compliment is indicative of double-mindedness.

If we are to get along with people we must reconcile ourselves to disappointments in those whom we have trusted. This is the source of one of the greatest temptations that can come in life, the betrayal of one's confidence by a friend. Suppose, however, being completely upset over a betrayed confidence, we set about to injure the person betraying us? We end only in doing ourselves the more harm.

If we establish a reputation for being "touchy" and supersensitive, we miss the helpful criticism that should come to us normally. "Touchy" people are left alone to reap a lonely harvest of their own faults and failures. Of course criticism is sometimes quite unjustifiable. In this event we must turn a deaf ear to it, not allowing ourselves to be upset.

Capacity for making friends is a factor that must not be overlooked if we are to get along with people. "He that would have friends must show himself friendly." That friendship that warms the hearts of men, making the sun shine for them a little brighter, that carries men along the paths of trust and mutual understanding—that friendship, let it be repeated, does not come unsought. The world will let you sit alone beside the road under your own little gourd vine if you fail to move out and make friends with others.

It is quite possible for a man to get along with others, yet not with himself. I have met many people in life who were in a constant taurmoil and confusion as they fell out with themselves. None of us is free from making mistakes which are a source of embarrassment to us. The Apostle Paul exhorts us not to allow the mistakes and failures of the past to keep us so disturbed that we lose the victory for the present. He admonishes us to forget those things which are behind, and to press forward to the things that are ahead. Those who have not yet learned to get along with themselves will find life's burden growing greater with each passing year. The harvest of an irritable temper, a grouchy disposition, a "touchy" and sensitive nature, will embarrass us at each turn of life's road.

Jesus Christ is the supreme example of getting along with men. He loved people. He was their friend. To the woman with a stain of impurity upon her life, He said: "Go, and sin no more." When His disciples wanted to pull fire down from heaven upon certain ones who were not preaching according to standard, Jesus said, "Forbid them not, he that is not against me is for me."

Jesus Christ is a friend who can help us to be friendly. With Him enthroned in our hearts and lives we have the greatest force of all to help us get along with people. He who himself endured such contradictions and criticisms knows how to strengthen us in the hours of conflict with other people. He who was rich in forgiveness toward those who crucified Him can impart a like spirit to those who follow Him. He who said, "I am the way, the truth, and the life," can help us live victoriously with other people.

THE BANISHMENT OF DEFEAT

CHAPTER IX.

It is the desire of every one to make a success in life. A sense of defeat is one of the most depressing experiences that can come to us. While it is true that our failures are often our most difficult hurdles, they can be used as stepping stones to higher things. They need not keep us down.

One of the very first factors leading to success is the ability to maintain the forward and upward look. It is a grave mistake to gaze too long on our past failures. When we look at the past, it should be to correct our failures rather than to meditate upon them until they exercise an increasingly discouraging influence over us. The forward look of the Apostle Paul is set forth in the words, "reaching forth unto those things which are before." Paul lived in anticipation of the fact that his best days were yet ahead. With regard to the best days of one's life, some people make the mistake of maintaining the backward look. But past days are gone forever; surely the days that are ahead can be for us the richest and most challenging of our lives. But that depends on us.

The upward look of the apostle is further described in the words: "I press toward the mark for the prize of the high calling of God in Christ Jesus." Paul looked to a higher power for divine guidance. He realized that there are certain elements in life over which we have no control. There is, of course, much that we may do through the exercise of will power, but after will power has achieved its utmost, there is still need for the divine hand to guide and direct us in the way of life. The forward, upward look is an essential factor for success in any field of human endeavor.

Our mental attitude is a large determining factor in success. An attitude of defeatism can never bring success. Those who would succeed in life must culitivate a spirit of optimism, must act as if it were impossible to fail. Should failure come to such they meet it with fortitude and somehow turn it to their own advantage. A cheerful, optimistic frame of mind toward our work always releases new energy to facilitate achievement. Work under such conditions is never drudgery. Instead of feeling driven to the task one finds himself irresistibly drawn toward it.

The spirit of courageous optimism, so essential to success, may be sorely tempted. There is, for instance, the temptation to daydream. to substitute wishful thinking for realistic action. The daydreamer deteriorates to the point where he has only a wishbone. He is ever dreaming of things and of goals which never materialize; and that because he never puts forth any effective efforts to reach them. There are people who fall into the delusion that they may hypnotize themselves into success. Real success comes to grips with reality. Daydreams may for the time being bring about a state of delightful intoxication. But just as the after effect of acloholic drunkenness is morbidity and gloom, even so the aftermath of delightful mental intoxication is often abject melancholia.

Important as it is that we act as if failure

were impossible, it is equally essential that we make no extravagant affirmations such as, "I cannot fail," or "I am successful in all I do." We must guard against a spirit that might be interpreted as proud and boastful. A proud and boastful spirit focuses attention upon the self. Real success is never self-centered. All true success is "other-centered."

Jesus stated a fundamental law for successful living when He said: "It is more blessed to give than to receive." It is a very narrow and restricted interpretation which limits the meaning of these words of Jesus to money. There are greater values in life than money. It is important to give money, for money in a very proper sense may represent our personality. But in these words, Christ in a fuller sense meant: it is blessed to be "other-centered," not "self-centered." If our labors are to be truly successful, we must always be thinking in terms of the service which we may be able to render to others. We are to think of life in terms of investing our talents for the good of others. When we so invest them in and for others to the limit of our capacity, we succeed. Just in proportion as we fall short of this goal, we become failures. This fact should prove an incentive to every one to reach out for larger achievements.

Some one has said: "Success depends on a plus condition of mind and body, on power of work, on courage." This plus condition may come through religious faith. It is illustrated in the fishermen of Galilee who turned to follow Jesus of Nazareth. They became something more than the other fishermen of their day. They became supermen because their lives were transformed by the touch of the Super-Person. It was the plus that counted. A genuine religious awakening coming through the new birth in Christ acts so dynamically upon the personality as to make a man a new creature. To that plus condition of mind and heart found in the Christian faith there must be added the power of work and of courage.

The aggravating sit-down strikes which we had in industry a few years ago seem to have somewhat subsided; but mental and spiritual sit-down strikes are still in vogue,

The temptation to laziness is as old as the human race. The alibis for laziness are so plausible these days that we may actually be "lazy with distinction," as one writer has put it. But laziness with distinction means failure just as much as laziness with disgrace.

To work, the virtue of courage must also be added. When the disciples had toiled all night as fishermen on the Sea of Galilee, and had taken no fish, Jesus commanded them to courage: "Launch out into the deep." In obedience to this command, they took a good catch of fish. Defeat was turned to success. Unto all who have met with any failure, Jesus says: "Launch out into the deep." So then, if we would banish defeat in the spiritual life, we must maintain that forward, upward look which transcends the temptation to pessimism, daydreaming, and self-centeredness. We must acquire through Christ that plus condition of mind and body which energizes to real work and courageous service.

THE OLD PATHS

CHAPTER X.

There is a widespread desire among people in this age to be "up-to-date." We have a kind of mania for "the very latest thing." This quest for the "up-to-date" is normal and legitimate when confined to proper limits.

Yet in a world in which startling discoveries and inventions are being announced every day, all making for human progress and the relief of suffering and the prolongation of life, there are also a number of things, not new, which are essential to life. They are old. Some of them are older than the race itself. These things are just as essential for the life of man today as they were in the remote past.

Many kinds of beverages have been devised by modern man. One of these is coffee. The Greeks and the Romans never heard of it. Coffee was unknown in England until about 300 years ago. In more recent times we have developed a score or more of soft drinks. Some of them are now very popular, and are the source of large incomes to their manufacturers. But these modern drinks have not done away with the necessity of water. Water is as essential to the life of man today as it was to the inhabitants of the earth five thousand years ago.

During the past fifty years many improvements have been made in the field of artificial illumination. It is a long way from the tallow candle with which the pioneers of America lighted their log cabins, to the splendid illumination of electric lights which we have in our homes today. We have light schemes, colors, and displays which were unknown to our fathers. But this vast improvement in illumination has in no way done away with the necessity for sunlight. The sun is just as essential to the life of the world today, as it was to the people upon the earth three thousand years before Christ. Medical men tell us that the sun is the health factory of the universe.

So amid all of our progress, and all of our mad rush for the things which are new and "up-to-date," there are some things which are old and abiding, to which we must ever be turning with the same confidence and urgency as did the people of long ago. Today doctors are requiring their patients to get more sunlight. It is still necessary to turn to the sun with its curative power for the prolongation of life.

In recent years we have had considerable agitation and propaganda relative to the necessity of a new religion, a new theology, a new approach to religion to meet the needs of modern man. The slogans and shibboleths of such have, of course, been in keeping with many of the campaign shibboleths of progress and development. God has told us, however, through His prophet Jeremiah, that there are certain "old paths" that are essential to the highest spiritual and moral development of any people. There are things in the spiritual and moral world that are even more fixed and even more enduring than are the things of the physical universe.

The conditions which prevailed in Judah at the time God commanded His children to return to the old paths is described in the sixth chapter of Jeremiah. The people had forsaken God, and had turned to the idols of the world. In the 7th verse of the 6th chapter of this book, we read: "As a fountain casteth out her waters, so she casteth out her wickedness; violence and spoil is heard in her; before me continually is grief and wounds." In the 13th verse of the chapter are the words: "For from the least of them even unto the greatest of them every one is given to covetousness; and from the prophet even unto the priest every one dealeth falsely." And again in the 15th verse: "were they ashamed when they committed abomination? Nay, they were not at all ashamed, neither could they blush; there they shall fall among them that fall; at the time that I visit them they shall be cast down, saith the Lord." These verses describe the state of violence and spoil that prevailed in Judah. The fountain of wickedness was running at floodtide. The people were given to covetousness; even the prophets and the priests had fallen into such sin that they dealt falsely with the people.

The people were not ashamed of their abominations and their wickedness. The expression, "neither could they blush," describes the prodigality of this wicked age. One of the sad characteristics of our own age is that there is no longer a blush at the widespread prevalence of wickedness, intemperance, and licentiousness. A melancholy sign of the decadence of this age is the large number of women who have lost the faculty to blush. The moral sense of the nation has been deadened and blunted. We have lost, in a large measure, the power to protest, and to raise a voice against the evils of our day. We have fallen into that dangerous habit of saying: "Oh, well, everybody's doing it. Why be concerned about such conditions?" It was to the people of an age similar to our own that God spoke the message, saying: "Stand ye in the ways and see, and ask for the old paths. . . . and ye shall find rest for your souls." But they said, "We will not walk therein."

The wickedness of the people is further described in the 20th verse of this sixth chapter: "To what purpose cometh there to me incense from Sheba, and the sweet cane from a far country? Your burnt offerings are not acceptable nor your sacrifices sweet unto me." The wickedness of the people is again exposed in the 28th verse: "They are all grievous revolters, walking with slanders: they are brass and iron; they are all corrupters."

What *are* the old paths to which God directs His people? They are enumerated in the sixth and seventh chapters of Jeremiah. The first mentioned is the old path of spiritual concern. It gives birth to prayer and fasting for the people who have turned their backs upon God. The 20th verse of the 6th chapter reads: "O daughter of my people, gird thee with sackcloth, and wallow thyself in ashes: make thee mourning as for an only son, most bitter lamentation: for the spoiler shall suddenly come upon us." This is an exhortation similar to that which was given to the king of Ninevah when he was warned by the prophet Jonah that Ninevah was to be destroyed. In that instance the prayers of the people changed the destiny of the city, and the city was saved. The inhabitants of Judah likewise were proud and haughty, negligent of worship and of the commandments of God. Verse 14 says of her prophets ond priests: "They have healed also the hurt of the daughter of my people slightly, saying, Peace, peace; when there is no peace." The exhortation to return to this first "old path" is greatly needed today.

Very few people are carrying any great burden. Very few are deeply concerned. Only a few spend periods in travailing prayer. We can never lift the load of the present hour with the routine praying many Christians are accustomed to. Somebody must become alarmed. Somebody must carry the heavy load. There must be a concern sufficient to spend much time in prayer, pleading about the conditions that confront us. David in the Psalms repeatedly says, "I cried unto the Lord." This statement indicates an earnestness, a passion, a deep concern, an agony of soul that would not be denied an answer from God. When people are in earnest and "praying clear through" until the Holy Spirit witnesses to the fact of answered prayer, something begins to happen; in fact, something has already happened when such praying takes place, although some time may elapse before the answer to the prayer is fully realized.

We need to return to the old path of prayer in the home, where the Bible is read daily, and where prayer is offered about the family altar. The homes of our forefathers where prayer was frequently heard furnished a course in Christian education far surpassing the offerings of the modern Christian education curriculum. It made impressions that live on through the years. We should return to the old path of prayer which Daniel trod when he kept his window open toward Jerusalem, praying three times a day, even when the decree had gone forth jeopardizing his life.

No great spiritual awakening has ever come without the background of much prayer. It is a good motto which reads: "Prayer changes things." The world needs to be changed. It is in a state of chaos and confusion. There is much in the church that needs to be changed. The deadness and formality of the modern church need to be changed until the church becomes aglow with spiritual power. When we again travel the old paths of prayer, praying until we touch the throne of God, the changes so much needed in our individual lives will begin to come to pass.

Without divine aid, our nation is headed for increasing confusion and distress. It is high time that we turned again to those old paths of simple faith and humble reliance upon God and His holy word which characterized the founding fathers of our great nation. We shall not in any manner be beating a retreat when we return to the old paths of their faith; we shall rather be making a great advance, in which we shall have the guidance and protection of God in spreading God's kingdom among men and in realizing a glorious new destiny of faith and freedom.

FAITH FOR THE STORMS

CHAPTER XI

The faith that weathers successfully the storm lays hold of the willingness of God to manifest His presence and to support in meeting every human need. No righteous cause or righteous person has ever sailed a stormless sea.

The Christian Church encountered storms of persecution from the very beginning. Jesus warned His disciples in advance that they would encounter severe opposition and grievous persecution. Paul, the greatest of the apostles, seemed to encounter more storms than any other disciple of his day. In II Corinthians, chapter eleven, verses 24 through 27, he describes some of these storms:

"Of the Jews five times received I forty stripes save one. Thrice was I beaten with rods, once was I stoned, thrice I suffered shipwreck, a night and a day I have been in the deep. In journeying often, in perils of waters, in perils of robbers, in perils by mine own countrymen, in perils by the heathen, in perils in the city, in perils in the wilderness. in perils in the sea, in perils among false brethren; in weariness and painfulness. in watching often, in hunger and thirst, in fastings often, in cold and nakedness." At the conclusion of this list of hardships the apostle adds these words: "If I must needs glory, I will glory of the things which concern mine infirmities."

Paul had a faith that enabled him to weather every storm. We should ever bear in mind that every command of God to go forward involves battles to be fought, testings to be met, and storms to be encountered. These trials make possible perpetual conquests. The apostle for many years had a burning desire to see Rome. Even as a prisoner in bonds, he rejoiced greatly in his privilege as a Roman citizen to appeal to Caesar, for thus would he see Rome. His journey there was a long and perilous one. It was during this voyage in the midst of a dreadful storm, that Paul prayed and fasted until the angel of the Lord stood by, giving him the blessed assurance that though the ship would be wrecked, all lives would be saved.   Paul gave the captain and his panic-stricken crew the assurance of his answered prayer.   He thus addressed them, tempest-tossed for fourteen days, "I exhort you to be of good cheer; for there shall be no loss of any man's life, but of the ship.   There stood by me this night the angel of God, whose I am, and whom I serve, saying, Fear not, Paul, thou must be brought before Caesar; so God hath given thee all of them that sail with thee.   Therefore, sirs, be of good cheer: for I believe God that it shall be even as it was told me."

Paul, the man of prayer, became the captain of the ship.   His message in the midst of the storm was, "Be of good cheer."   His testimony was a fulfillment of the Scriptures: "This is the victory that overcometh the world, even our faith."   At last he entered Rome according to the Word of the Lord, which came to him in the prison at Jerusalem, saying: "Be of good cheer, Paul, for as thou hast testified of me in Jerusalem, so must thou bear witness also at Rome."

Paul not only came to Rome, but with that

same indomitable faith and courage he showed himself there to be quite prepared to face whatever else life held for him. "For I am now ready to be offered, and the time of my departure is at hand. I have fought a good fight, I have finished my course, I have kept the faith: henceforth there is laid up for me a crown of righteousness which the Lord, the righteous judge, shall give to me in that day: and not to me only, but unto all of them also that love his appearing."

During World War II, reports came from all parts of the world of men in perplexity and distress turning to the way of faith. The heroic American soldiers who defended Bataan sent back word to the homeland, "There are no atheists in fox holes." Newspaper correspondents reported typical scenes of men reading their Bibles during temporary lulls while operating anti-aircraft guns. Some four hundred men on a transport ship asked a Christian worker to address them, prefacing their invitation with the request, "We are not interested in being entertained, but tell us how to die."

Numerous Russian prisoners captured in the battle with Finland were in possession of smuggled Bibles. Even in Soviet Russia reports came of Chaplains being permitted to enter the front-line trenches of battle to give the comfort and solace of religion. The chaplains of the army and navy of the United States literally clamored for Bibles to give to the men in the service. A survey of military camps reveals that men in the service attended religious services in larger proportion than did civilians.

On a Sunday morning during World War II, a father placed in my hand a telegram. The telegram was to the father from the War Department in Washington announcing that his son, a Captain in the Air Corps, was missing. On the telegram the father had added a note requesting the congregation to sing, "Holy, Holy, Holy, Lord God Almighty;" he also asked for special prayer. That father was in all of the services on that Lord's day with a heavy heart, but with a faith that did not waver in the midst of his sorrow. In the Sunday evening service a few minutes before I entered my pulpit he stood and gave a testimony concerning the comfort of his faith, and of assurance in the midst of sorrow of the presence of the living God.

Without the victory of faith, there is no hope for us as individuals and as nations, and no hope for the world. Only the victory of faith can lead us safely through the storms, which at times turn the whole earth into a fearful tempest.

SECRET POWER

CHAPTER XII

Jesus gave two commandments shortly before He left the world. One was "go," the other was "tarry." They are paradoxical the one to the other, the first being the complement of the second.

The tarrying was to the end that they be fully equipped for the going. They could go farther and faster by having waited for "the promise of the Father." They could save time by what might appear to some as wasting time, for tarrying is no squandering of time. Some people feel too busy to tarry. They rush so rapidly from one thing to another that they do not find time to heed this command of the Master. Others resent the searchlight of heaven being turned upon the inner life of the soul. They are tempted to run from what they see when this light is upon them. But to ignore those things that God is trying to show us is not only to blind ourselves to the reality of our spiritual need, but also to make impossible our baptism with the Holy Spirit.

There was a very deep spiritual need on the part of the disciples to whom Jesus gave the command: "Tarry until ye be endued with power from on high." That need is common to disciples of every age. It grows out of the essentially human nature of man. The twelve were subject to all the frailties and weaknesses of a fallen humanity. They are representative of men of various temperaments and dispositions. Their weaknesses are clearly revealed in the gopsel story. Impetuosity, quick temper, unholy ambition, and slowness to believe were characteristic of their nature, bearing testimony to their spiritual need. The tarrying in the upper room threw into bold relief these unChristlike symptoms, showing them as obstructions to the fulness of power that comes with the baptism of the Holy Spirit.

The record clearly shows the disciples to be largely self-centered before the upper room experience. They were thinking of themselves, and of the place which they would have in the earthly kingdom which they expected Jesus to establish. They were ready to crown Him as a King. A selfish attitude was manifest in the plea of two of the disciples for first places, one on the right hand and the other on the left hand, in the Lord's anticipated earthly kingdom. When people are self-centered they demand much attention; when they forget self, they share.

The unselfish life lives by giving. The selfish life lives by receiving. When Jesus said: "It is more blessed to give than to receive," He stated a fundamental principle which reaches far beyond the mere giving of money. We often think of this statement as referring to what we put into the collection plate at church, or what we give to the poor. But the principle taught here is applicable to the whole of life. It is more blessed to give kindness than to receive kindness. It is more blessed to give praise than to receive praise. It is more blessed to pray for others than to be prayed for. It is more blessed to visit somebody that needs encouragement than to be visited with encouragement. It is more blessed to give sacrificial love for others than to receive the benefits of sacrificial love for oneself. After

Pentecost, the disciples rejoiced in the privilege of suffering for the Master. They found their joy, not in places of ease, but in having the privilege of giving themselves in sacrifice for Him and others.

The tarrying necessary to receive this upper room experience may involve an inner struggle. The tempter will put forth every effort to cause us to quit tarrying, to try to make us forget those unholy things standing in the way of our highest spiritual good. Yet the operating room experience is necessary. Some physicial ailments require the surgeon's knife. The patient recognizes the malady, and wants to get rid of it, but he dreads the operation. Nothing less than the surgery of the upper room can meet the deepest moral and spiritual need of the disciples of Christ. The Old Man of sin whence spring evil dispositions, attitudes, tempers, ambitions, and irritable words, does not submit easily to divine surgery. Many devout Christians know that they are in need of spiritual surgery. They tell you frankly that they anticipate a day when it will take place, yet they put off the operation from year to year. God's time for spiritual surgery is now. With the disciples in the upper room we too may experience even in this life the complete cleansing of our hearts from all sin.

This upper room baptism with the Holy Spirit also imparted power. Jesus said: "Ye shall receive power after that the Holy Ghost is come upon you." We need power to stand in strength and security. In the first stages of erecting a great building the structure must be held up with many props. But the day comes when these props are torn away, and the building stands of itself, a thing of beauty, strength, and security. Children must be well propped. Babes in Christ take a lot of props, props from the preacher, props from the Sunday school teacher, props from other Christians. If the props should be taken away, they are not strong enough to stand alone. It is the work of the Holy Spirit to impart to every child of God the strength to stand without props, in strength and security.

STARS IN THE VALLEY OF DISCOURAGEMENT

CHAPTER XIII

Life is a journey that leads across vast plains and tablelands, over high mountains, and through many valleys. It offers many sloughs of despondency, many valleys of discouragement. Yet there are stars in God's heavens that are ever shining to guide the pilgrims of earth on their eternity-bound journey.

To the eye of faith, these stars are more real than the physical stars that dot the heavens at night. They were shining before any of the heavenly bodies were placed in their orbits, before the morning stars sang together and shouted with joy at the handiwork of their Creator. From the first misty morning of time until now, they have evoked songs in the night; they have lightened the burdens of weary-worn travelers; and they have restored the fallen in the ways of righteousness. From the beginning the light of these stars has stretched as a bow of hope across the sky for the despondent and the despairing.

The astronomers have given names to the stars in the physical firmament. And not unknown to us are the names of some of of those stars in the spiritual firmament which shed light upon our pathway in the valley of discouragement. One of them is named hope. On life's journey we are to be ever hopeful, always planning for the best. The light of human experience through the ages teaches plainly the futility of pessimism. Yet pessimism is one of the most common temptations in life.

As far back as we are able to go in the pages of ancient civilization, we find its record. An old Assyrian tablet dated 2800 B.C. has the following inscription: "Our earth is degenerate in these latter days. There are signs that the world is speedily coming to an end. Children no longer obey their parents. Every man wants to write a book. The end of the world is evidently approaching."

The enemy of the souls of men would have them believe that there is no divine providential care watching over their destiny. Martin Luther once yielded to pessimism.

He had been fasting for several days and was reduced to a state of extreme melancholy when one morning his wife came into the room dressed in mourning. Luther looked at his wife in astonishment, making inquiry: "Why are you dressed in mourning?" She replied: "God is dead, and I have come in to help you mourn over Him." Her action broke the spell of Luther's pessimism.

Discouraged hearts should find much cheer in the Bible. If ever a man had a right to feel pessimistic surely it was Joshua when he faced the task of leading the children of Israel into the promised land. The great leader, Moses, was dead, and the new leader felt his inadequency. But God still lived. Three times did God in the first chapter of the book that bears his name urge the new leader: "be strong and of a good courage." Consider also an instance or two from the New Testament. When the disciples in the midst of the storm at sea despaired of life, Christ spoke to them: "It is I: be not afraid." Again, before leaving this world, He urged them saying: "Let not not your heart be troubled." His message to His disciples was always one of cheer and comfort. It is not God's purpose that any one should have a discouraged attitude toward life. God desires His people to be abounding in the fulness of joy and gladness.

The best of men, however, are tempted to discouragement. Those who have found the better way of life will pass victoriously through these periods of temptation, which do not last when resisted. If we surrender to periods of discouragement, however, they will not only come more frequently but like some malignant growth they will also in the end prove fatal. When tempted to discouragement, we should remember that no matter how dark the night and how overcast the sky, the stars though unseen are still shining. Their light is always there when faith reaches beyond the clouds.

Another star in the spiritual firmament is the star of thanksgiving. Jesus set the great example of giving thanks in darkest night. In Paul's first letter to the Corinthians are these words concerning Jesus: "The Lord Jesus, the same night in which he was betrayed, took bread, and when he had given thanks, he brake it." In that hour when sin, hatred, and evil were at floodtide, beating against His soul, Jesus gave thanks.

Ever shining to guide the discouraged is yet another star—the star of faith—faith that acts in the present according to the light it has of the future. When discouragements come out of the past and the present, it is well that we lift our eyes to the future and live now by faith in the light of that future. While the shadow of the cross was falling across His pathway, Jesus made provisions for the future of His little band of disciples. Thinking of His decease, He told them what to do in remembrance of Him. Did He not inaugurate the Holy Sacrament in that dark hour when the black shadows of the cross were already beginning to fall across His pathway?

When we live in the past, brooding over the failures and disappointments of yesterday, we are incapacitated for the tasks of today. We should never lose the lure of the tomorrow. It is true that the tomorrows of this life come to an end. But on the last day of this earthly life, there is the tomorrow of a life beyond and it is our faith in this glorious tomorrow that must steer our course today. Let us not fail to lift our eyes unto the hills of the future, for there is the stimulus for victory in the present.

But the brightest of all the stars that shine in the firmament of a despondent and discouraged world is the Star of Bethlehem. This is the Bright and Morning star that came out of David, the glorious hope foretold by the prophets and seers. It is the light of this Star that gives meaning to all the other stars in the firmament. The Bright and Morning Star will drive away the darkness. He banishes storms with the beck of His hand. He calms the fevered brow with a soothing word. He comforts the sorrowing with the touch of His hand. If you have fallen into the Valley of Discouragement, rise to your feet, lift up your eyes, and take the upward look at the eternal stars of God shining for you from the beginning of time. In the light of the glorious Morning Star your path, however dark it be, will light up, and peace and victory shall be yours.

THE CURE FOR WORRY

CHAPTER XIV

When Jesus said: "Take no thought for the morrow," He meant, "Be not overly anxious for the morrow." Jesus never taught that we were to live unconcerned about the future. He did teach us that we were not to allow worry to enter our lives to such a degree as to rob us of the present and cheat us of the future.

It is quite easy for us to justify ourselves for the multitude of worries that beset us. Yet we delude ourselves into believing that the things over which we worry are peculiar to our lives alone. We forget that in each life are problems and difficulties inviting worry. The Bible says in this connection, "There hath no temptation taken you but such as is common to man." It is characteristic of the enemy of our souls to engage us in worry and thus start us staggering toward defeat. The story is told that on one occasion Satan sent one of his agents to tempt a certain man in the world. He said to this demon: "You go up to earth and get that man discouraged." The demon flew off to the world, and lighting upon the shoulder of this man, said: "You are discouraged." The man replied: "No, I am not." Again the demon said: "You are discouraged." The man replied, "No, I am not." Again the demon said, "You are discouraged." The man still replied, "No, I am not." After this failure, the demon flew back to Satan to give a report, saying that he was unable to discourage the man. Satan again ordered the demon to return and get the man discouraged. The demon returned, and again tried the same formula. But again each time the man said: "No, I am not discouraged." The evil spirit once more returned to report. Satan asked: "Did you get the man discouraged?" The demon replied, "No, I could not get him discouraged, and I am now discouraged myself."

You can never win with the frown of worry, but you can win with the smile of encouragement. If the enemy can dump you in the Slough of Despondency he has you whipped so long as you remain in that slough. The only way you can ever win is to get out, throw your shoulders back, turn your face upward, and begin marching with the upward, forward look.

This matter of not worrying does not mean that our eyes are to be blinded to things which should give us concern. When Jesus told us not to be anxious about the morrow, He meant that we are not so to worry about tomorrow that we are incapacitated for today. There is a false and a true optimism. A false optimism has blind eyes toward the realities of life. It takes the short-cut, and denies the existence of things as they are. A genuine optimism always takes into account the stern realities of life. It faces discouraging circumstances, but it does not allow them to overwhelm the soul to the point of defeat. Since we shall need our strongest resources to meet these handicapping circumstances, we must not allow the deadly poison of worry to infect us, neutralizing our possibilities.

What are some of the things about which people worry? Many worry over a lost possession. It may be a lost love, a lost opportunity, a loss in business, a loss in health, or a loss in prestige and position. We could

The Cure For Worry   103

go on enumerating a long list of losses over
which people ordinarily worry. When we
give consideration to our losses we must ever
bear in mind that in connection with every
loss there may be some new gain which, at
the time, is not apparent, but which will certainly be revealed if we manifest the spirit
of patience and trust. For every closed door
there may come some new open door; and
often the door that opens will hold more for
us than the door that remained closed.

One of the greatest disappointments in
the life of the Apostle Paul was his dis-
covery that the door was closed to him to
preach in Jerusalem. In Jerusalem he had
been a member of the great Sanhedrin. In
finding the Christ, he fully expected that a
great opportunity would be given him to
proclaim the message of the Saviour to his
former friends and acquaintances in that
city. It was indeed a stunning blow that
this door should be absolutely closed against
him. With that door closed, however, a
door was opened to him to preach the gospel
in Rome, the metropolis of the world. The
results of his witness in that city testify to

the unerring strategy of the Holy Spirit.

John Bunyan's years of imprisonment in Bedford jail closed the door against his preaching to the people during that period, but it opened the door for him to write "Pilgrim's Progress" a work that immortalized his name, a literary masterpiece with a circulation larger than any other book except the Bible.

Every loss can bring a new experience into our lives to make us stronger. The loss, however, which casts us into the Slough of Despondency is likely to become irreparable. While it is true that many of the losses in life are of such a nature that they can never be regained, it is also true that we can gain something even bigger than the recovery of the loss—victory in disappointment.

Another common cause for worry is the past. We must learn to turn our backs upon the past in the matter of worry. There are things that have occurred in our past for which we should repent, for which we should make amends as far as possible. But having repented and solicited the help of God, we have the assurance that God no longer remembers the past. This is a matter for our encouragement. If God does not remember the past, after He has forgiven us, then certainly we should not worry over the past. God has promised that He will forgive us our sins, and remember them against us no more for ever. He will never bring anything up out of the past for our condemnation when we turn to Him for forgiveness. So far as God is concerned our lives are as though the sin had never been committed. Does not the Apostle Paul exhort us to forget things that are behind, and press toward the mark of the high calling which is in Christ Jesus our Lord? It was the sin of looking back that caused Lot's wife to turn into a pillar of salt. The sin of looking back has caused many people to turn into pillars of discouragement, a condition just as fatal as being turned into a pillar of salt.

Another common cause for discouragement is the evil of other people. David said: "Fret not thyself because of evil doers." This exhortation not to fret about evil doers does not mean that we are to condone evil doing. It does not mean that we are to keep our eyes blinded to the evils of men about us. Our eyes are ever to be open to the evils of men, but we are not to allow these evils to discourage us. This is an age when evil is holding large sway, when sin is holding high carnival throughout the world. But in the face of discouraging circumstances all about us, there is an anchorage of peace and victory for every soul. While others may travel the evil roads, it is possible for us to travel the better way. While others live in rebellion against God, it is possible for us to live in humble submission to His will. While sin and impurity are the order of the day about us, it is possible for us to be pure within.

What is the secret of a life of victory over worry and discouragement? This secret is worth more than all the gold of ancient Croesus, and all the wealth of a modern Rockefeller. The secret of a life that is victorious over worry is a life of faith and trust in God, and in His well-beloved Son, Jesus Christ. Jesus sets the supreme example of a life without worry. His life was as calm as a June morning, and as even in its tempo as the placid waters of a mountain lake. The secret was the secret of prayer and intercession. His secret was the secret of rendering helpful service to others, always going about doing good. This secret of faith and inner trust means daily communion with the heavenly Father who can control the storm and the tempest. It is the secret of victory over worry and fear. Jesus said: "Let not your heart be troubled; ye believe in God, believe also in me."

FAITH HEALING

CHAPTER XV

The quest for healing remedies for ailments of body and mind is as old as the race
itself. Since the first man lost his pristine
purity in the Garden of Eden, man has
struggled with the thorn of physical affliction. He is ever on the quest for elixirs,
tonics, and remedies to relieve pain and suffering, and to increase longevity.

The apothecary stores have many tonics
for the body. But these tonics are spas-
modics; they come and they go. Comparatively few of the standard brands of fifty
years ago remain on sale in the drug store
of the present day. Some of us can recall
nationally advertised tonics of twenty-five
years ago that are no longer advertised. If
some of these which formerly received large
space in national publicity had measured
up to their claim, they would still be big
sellers.

There is one remedy for man's afflictions
that has endured through the years. Many

centuries old, it is still being used, and with the same results. This remedy has outlived not only all other remedies; it has also survived empires and civilizations. It is the mightiest tonic in the world—faith. Faith-healing is as old as the race. In recent years it has commanded a growing recognition from medical authorities. An article by Dr. C. Raimer Smith appearing in the June '31 issue of Hygeia,* the official health magazine of the American Medical Association, gives due recognition to the place of faith in the cure of disease. A comment from the article is as follows: "Faith should not be deprecated. It has a great importance in the treatment of disease. But it takes faith plus work. Faith without works is dead." Meaning, of course, that the person who is sick should do all in his power to cure his condition in the light of the scientific medical findings of those who are investigating God's great laws of nature.

It is a well-established scientific fact that a large per cent of the ills of the human race are functional. Some medical authorities estimate that fifty per cent of our physical ills are such. They rise from inner mental conflicts which affect the nerves controlling certain organs of the body. Fright and deep grief affect the heart, the appetite, and the digestion. One of the main nerves stemming from the brain controls the secretion of gastric juice. Grief or worry may affect this nerve to the point where this secretion is inhibited, with the result that food will not digest. Under such strong emotionally-toned conditions there is probably nothing organically wrong with the stomach. The cure needed is not drugs. It is one having to do with the restoration of a calm and composed mind. If the nerve is affected by grief or worry, whatever relieves the disturbance will prove to be an effective remedy.

Other factors that affect the nerves to the extent of creating functional disorders are: domestic discord, anger, hatred, jealousy, and occupational maladjustment. These functional disturbances arising from nervous derangement may produce aches and pains in almost every part of the body. Medical men tell us that worry and grief may cause an oversecretion of hydro-chloric acid in the stomach, resulting in stomach ulcers; that an unhappy state of mind may produce insomnia, a poor appetite and irregular habits; and it may so lower physical vitality as to pave the way for tuberculosis and other maladies. A disease that is at first functional may become organic. In its functional stage it may be cured by relief from nervous tension. Once organic, however, the organs in question will also need to be treated.

We are not necessarily displaying a lack of faith when we call upon the doctor. We are but manifesting our faith in revealed secrets of God's healing power through natural remedies. All healing comes from God. The doctor is one medium of healing. He himself is not the healer but the administrator of the healing laws of God. The doctor, however, may be helpless without the aid of the faith which comes through prayer.

Deranged nerve conditions may be alleviated to a degree by the presence of certain persons. There is a healing influence and power in having certain relatives and friends visit us in times of sickness under certain conditions. The visit of a cheerful friend at the sick bed may have the stimulating effect of a tonic.

And what shall we say of the healing virtues to be found in the presence of Christ, the great Healer! Jesus Christ is the great tonic for depressed spirits and jangled nerves. It should not be difficult for us to believe that in the peace and joy that flows from His presence may be found healing for every kind of nervous disorder. That strength, joy, and patience which Christ can give is described by Paul in his Epistle to the Colossians: "Strengthened with all might, according to his glorious power, and to all patience and long-suffering with joyfulness." Faith seizes upon His willingness to heal and opens the clogged channel through which His healing power comes to meet our physical needs. Faith opens the bottle-neck and permits Christ's glorious power to bring healing to our broken bodies. Nor is Christ's healing power limited to functional diseases. He has been known to effect cures of organic diseases when the doctors have failed.

We can place no limit on faith's ability to appropriate the power of Him who said: "All power is given unto me in heaven and in earth." During His earthly ministry He demonstrated, in response to faith, His power in the healing of all manner of diseases. To the woman who suffered with an issue of blood for twelve years He said: "Thy faith hath made thee whole." Faith healing of course, demands a complete surrender of body, mind, and spirit unto Christ. The seeker of healing must commit his will to the will of Christ. Just as a broken connection will hinder the transmission of electric power from the powerhouse, so our connections with Him must be intact if we are to receive mental and physical healing from the infinite storehouse of God. So then the successful operation of our faith is conditional. It grows out of our relationship with Christ—one of unconditional surrender of the will.

*This publication has recently changed its title to "Today's Health."

HEALING THROUGH PRAYER

CHAPTER XVI

Prayer is no shortcut of escape to the Christian as is the bankruptcy law to the bankrupt. It is the disciplined way to reach the goal of the soul's sincere desire.

In prayer for healing, for example, the discipline is that of utilizing all the natural resources which God has placed at our command. The disciplined use of these facilities furnishes prayer with a background, and becomes the stepping stone of our faith. It is always a temptation to throw discretion to the winds by neglecting to use the natural means of healing and move along lines of least resistance. It is easier for some people to trust God than to exercise themselves in their own behalf. Such self-disciplinary measures are no means easy. For neglecting them many ailing men and women die prematurely. The temptation to follow the easy road, instead of the well-beaten winding path of discipline, brings its own reward.

I once knew a man with an affliction who was making encouraging gains in recovery, when two of his old friends eventually died of this same malady. He became discouraged and, deciding that further self-discipline was useless, he threw caution to the winds and began to pursue the course of least resistance. He paid little attention to his diet, neglected proper rest and exercise, and soon began to decline. It so happened in this particular case that an awakening came. Again he set out to lay hold of the natural resources that God had placed at his disposal. He began to pray, to honor God with his substance, and to attend the services of the church. This awakening to discipline was the beginning of a marked improvement in his physical condition.

Not only must we have discipline as a background for prayer, but the very habit of prayer itself requires discipline. It is easy to neglect the prayer life. The praying of many people is spasmodic. They pray by spells forgetting that prayer life which carries in it the elements of healing is a daily disciplined prayer life. Is it not passing strange that we should talk about everything and everybody and neglect to talk to God? We read the latest item in the news instead of seeking the latest news from heaven. We talk to friends and neighbors by the hour, neglecting to talk to God for even a few minutes. Oh, that we might realize the riches for every one of us in this God-appointed exercise of the soul. The more we pray the stronger we become. In proportion to our negligence is the dissipation of our spiritual life.

Healing through prayer requires not only a disciplined prayer life. It necessitates disciplined attitudes—the attitude of forgiveness, for instance. An unforgiving spirit harbored in the heart is an impediment to answered prayer. God has said that if we do not forgive we cannot be forgiven. Nor, in such a condition, can we expect His healing touch through prayer. Jesus teaches that when we bring our gift to the altar and remember that our brother has aught against us, we should first go and be reconciled to our brother. An unforgiving spirit clogs the channel through which the healing grace of God flows to the souls and bodies of men. This channel must be opened before the healing waters of divine grace can flow freely to meet our needs.

Another attitude essential to healing prayer is open-mindedness toward God and His ability to change the conditions of the body. It is an established fact that body conditions may be radically c h a n g e d through anger, fear, and excitement. Some years ago, the newspapers in big headlines carried the story of a man in a hospital in Brazil who had been paralyzed for years, unable to walk. One day a huge snake suddenly crawled into his hospital room. The fright of the paralyzed man was such that it affected his body. He jumped out of bed, fleeing from the room. The news reports were that the doctors pronounced him cured. An occurrence such as this is in the eyes of many so strange as to be incredible. Yet in its infancy so was radio, so was x-ray, and so was television. If we are to have the healing touch of prayer our minds must be open and appreciative of the fact that prayer may bring about a greater change in the human body for good than anger, fear, or excitement may bring for evil.

Anger is a deadly attitude which must be swept from our lives if we are to have healing through prayer. I cannot harbor anger in my heart toward any one and have the healing touch of God for my soul and body. Anger pours a poison into the blood stream. Its banishment helps to open the channel for the healing stream of God's grace. Another impediment often found clogging this channel of healing power is fear. Fear is rooted in self. When we forget ourselves we cease to be afraid.

A yielded confidence of all of our attitudes in submission to the will of God opens the way for the unhindered flow of the healing grace of God for every human need.

THE TONIC OF HUMOR

CHAPTER XVII

It is an old proverb: "A little fun now and then is good for the best of men." Another old adage is: "Grin and endure it." Still another: "Laugh and the world laughs with you; weep and you weep alone."

Some one has said: "God gave us humor to save us from going mad." In a world where nerves are racked and strained to the breaking point, humor is a tonic for relaxation. When a patient's nerves are about to snap, it is not uncommon for the doctor to recommend some form of relaxation. This treatment is necessary to keep intact the strained cables which hold life's load. Do not the builders of our great suspension bridges make allowance for contraction and expansion? The Golden Gate Bridge in California has a play of fourteen feet in which it may swing in time of storm. This seemingly vacillating rebound from the fixed order saves the bridge from wreckage when the storm breaks. Serving as a protection in the stresses of life, humor is the divine provision.   He who in the pressures of life retains a wholesome sense of humor will be the last in life's casualty list.

Alfred Tennyson wrote: "I dare not tell you how high I rate humor, which is generally most fruitful in the highest and most solemn human spirit.   Dante is full of it. Shakespeare, Cervantes, and almost all the greatest have been pregnant with this glorious power.   You will even find it in the gospel of Christ."

A few years ago the sandstorms in the dust bowl area of the United States became front page news in the daily press.   So devastating were they that sand penetrated even the motors of automobiles.   Sand on the pistons of an automobile destroys the motor in short order.   The reverses of life can be likened to the sandstorms of the dust bowl.   They send the grit of irritation into the soul.   That the pistons of life's machine may run smoothly, Christ gives us the solvent of humor to absorb this grit.   Humor maintains a buoyancy like a life preserver. And who among us is not the better fortified for this protection?

Although it is imperative that we duly consider the serious side of life, it is quite possible to take things too seriously. Here again humor comes as a joyful servant to save us from taking things too seriously, including ourselves. Robert Louis Stevenson said: "That people should laugh is a better preparation for life than many other things higher and better sounding in the world."

God's use of humor may be seen in the joyful playfulness of the young of both man and beast. I recall a pastoral call in a home where there was a two year old daughter. Since it was evening, the little girl had just donned her "nightie" for bed. The coming of a visitor into the home drove sleep from her eyes, and she turned into a frolic of laughter and play, making merriment for the whole household. She ran and leaped and dashed, and laughed in mirthful glee, breaking down the sobriety of the elders. Everybody caught the spirit of laughter that came like the waters of a gushing spring from the heart of this little one.

A young monkey in a round of humorous

antics will hold a crowd in rapt attention. A young puppy wears a smile upon his face, and he seems to carry a laugh in his wagging tail as he greets stranger and acquaintance alike with a bit of friendly sunshine. Leslie D. Weatherhead says: "He who has played with a baby or a monkey, a kitten or a puppy, has shared a joke with God."

With regard to humor, some people have a wrong conception of the Christian faith. The ascetic element in Christianity has overlooked the words of Jesus: "Be of good cheer; I have overcome the world." It is true that Jesus was a man of sorrows, and acquainted with grief; but it is also true that He carried in His heart joy and gladness. He expressed the desire that His joy might remain with His disciples. A laugh may be a faith thermometer, indicating that faith is still victorious. It is a mistake to assume that Jesus did not laugh. The fact that little children were attracted to Him suggests to us that the Master wore a smile. Children are not attracted to frowning adults; they are won by a smiling face.

The ascetic attitude in Christianity has

always been a temptation to some. The story has often been told of a young man who when dying sent for a deacon of the church to pray for him. The deacon came with great solemnity, and with solemn voice said to him: "Young man, it would seem that you are near death's door. Would you like to be a Christian?" The young man replied: "No, not if it makes me look as you do."

Divine humor, of course, is not buffoonery or cynical laughter. Men may foolishly laugh their way to ruin and perdition. Divine humor is as sweet as the scent of roses. It is as fresh and pure as the dew of a spring morning. It is as invigorating as the ocean breeze, distilling the impurities of the atmosphere. Every thing in life may be perverted and misused. And so with humor, it may be directed into evil channels. The humor that is divine is always a leaven for good.

It will help us maintain a proper spiritual perspective if we remember that the Bible over and over again makes statements similar to this: "The joy of the Lord shall be your strength." The prophet Joel sounds a note of lamentation at the absence of joy and gladness in the house of God, making two striking utterances in the first chapter of his prophecy: "Joy is withered away from the sons of men." And again, "Is not the meat cut off before our eyes, yea, joy and gladness from the house of our God?"

The misjudgment of the proper place of humor in the life of some Christians is well illustrated in a statement made nearly two centuries ago by Alexander Cruden, the noted Scottish Biblical scholar and compiler of the universally-acclaimed concordance. Cruden said: "To laugh is to be merry in a sinful manner." On the other hand, humor is to be recognized as a splendid tonic for the promotion of Christian optimism. It will strengthen us in fulfilling the exhortation of the Apostle Paul: "Rejoice in the Lord alway: and again I say, Rejoice." (Phil. 4:4).

THE FAR VIEW

CHAPTER XVIII

Paul's statement, "In everything give thanks" means that under all conditions and circumstances of life, we will find things for which to be thankful. The attitude of thanksgiving is preparatory for prayer. It is a preparation for constant and continual victory in our lives.

We have our trials and our problems. But in the midst of them we are to be thankful. Surely not for the trials! Rather because Christ is present with us in our trials.

We are to be thankful *in* afflictions, not *for* afflictions, but that we have a helper in the midst of our afflictions — One who stands beside us, One who is a comforter.

We are to be thankful *in* death, not *for* death, but thankful because we have One who is the conqueror over the grave, even Jesus Christ our Lord and Saviour, who conquered death.

On the occasion of the death of her celebrated husband, Mrs. Jonathan Edwards wrote a letter to her daughter, Mrs. Burr, in which she manifested an attitude of thanksgiving even in the midst of her great sorrow. The letter is dated April 3, 1758. Her husband had died on the 22nd of March. She wrote as follows:

"My very dear child: What shall I say? A holy and good God has covered us with a dark cloud. Oh, that we may kiss the rod and lay our hands on our mouths; the Lord has done it. He has made me adore His goodness that we had him so long. But my God lives and He has my heart. Oh, what a legacy my husband and your father has left us. We are all given to God and there I am and love to be. Your affectionate mother, Sarah Edwards."

Mrs. Edwards thanked God, not because the great preacher, her celebrated husband, had fallen sleep, but because she had One to sustain her in the midst of the great sorrow through which she was passing.

We fail so often in thanksgiving because we take the near view, the close view. We become involved with incidentals and fail to take the long view of God's eternal purposes. If we did, we would see the uplifted peaks and hills forming a far-flung horizon. Then we can evaluate the long sweep of God's providential dealings with a spirit of gratitude and thanksgiving.

I had a rich experience in Colorado Springs, visiting a patron of Asbury Theological Seminary, a man who walks with God as did Enoch of old. Over a period of years he had shown his interest in the work here by sending contributions to this institution; so when I went to that city, I looked him up. I was surprised. I expected to find a fairly good residence, perhaps a man with a good business. Instead, I found him living on the outskirts, on a little by-street, which was difficult to find. I searched for an hour or more before I found him. He was living, not in the substantial urban residence I had anticipated, but in a very small and humble cottage. In fact, it looked at first like a one-room cabin. I was later to discover that it contained two rooms.

I found living there a man, four-score and seven years of age, who had walked with God through the years. Instead of possessing a business with a comfortable income, he lived alone, an old age pensioner, doing his own cooking and housework. But he had a shine on his face.

I sat on his little porch while he, with radiant countenance, talked to me about passages of Scripture and his victory in Christ. Finally he said; "If you have time and are not in a hurry, I don't want to send you away empty-handed. I want to give you something."

I went inside. This aged servant of the Lord went into his other room to return with a contribution for the seminary that made my heart rejoice. His was like the giving of the widow, who gave more than all the rest when she gave her mite.

I returned to see this man of God on another morning and in our conversation he beckoned me with shining eyes: "Come out and see my view." When we stepped out on the little porch, there stretched out before us a grand panorama of uplifted mountains. Pike's Peak towered upon the western horizon. The sun was kissing the peak of this great giant of the rockies, and the

glory of the mountain seemed to be out on
dress parade. Such a view, it seemed to
me, I had not seen anywhere in all the world.

The man of God said: "Do you see my
view?" "Oh, yes, I see your view," was my
reply. Then the aged servant of the Lord
spoke with much feeling of the joy, peace,
and contentment that was in his soul. The
sublime spectacle before me almost eclipsed
my immediate surroundings. I forgot about
the cabin. I forgot about the small income.
I forgot about all those things that sug-
gested the poverty and hardship of my
friend's life. Here was a man who refused
to let his life be marred by things of lesser
consequences. Living in the higher realms,
with the far-flung vision, his life pulsated
with praise and thanksgiving.

God's challenge is in the far view. Here
only do we see the uplifted peaks of God's
grace—His infinite love and mercy. In this
view is the towering peak of Calvary, eloquent testimony to the atoning merits of
Jesus Christ our Lord; and beyond that
peak an empty tomb far above which is the
Christ seated upon the white horse, tran-

scending the din and fury of the world, riding in triumph, conquering and to conquer, until all kingdoms, principalities and powers shall be brought into subjection unto Him who is King of kings and Lord of lords and victor over all.

In the long view, when we hear what the centuries say as against the years, when we see God's purposes ripening, our understanding ears must need bow before Him in deep thanksgiving.

AT THE GATE OF HEAVEN

CHAPTER XIX

It was a beautiful day in June in a southern California city when I rang the doorbell of a modest cottage. It was a gracious greeting that Mrs. McPheeters and I received from the saintly woman who lived alone, and yet not alone, in the humble cottage. Only a few days previous, this handmaiden of the Lord had reached the ripe age of four-score and nine years. Her faculties were alert and the radiance of her countenance made one think of the shining face of Stephen.

On the occasion of her 89th birthday, people from several churches came to do her honor, including Methodists, Presbyterians Nazarenes and Catholics. The influence of her life had made such an impact upon the city that people of many faiths claimed her as their own. The gifts which these friends had left were all about the cottage as expressions of their love and admiration for a woman who had walked with the Lord in their midst.

131

When we were seated, we recognized immediately that we had been "made to sit together" in one of the "heavenly places in Christ Jesus." As the needle on the compass turns to the pole, so the conversation turned naturally to the things of the kingdom of God. The freshness of the words which fell from the lips of our gracious hostess was as the dew from heaven. We were made to realize that we had succeeded where Ponce de Leon had failed. We had found the fountain of perpetual youth in the life of one whose advanced years had failed to stamp the scars of age upon the inner spirit. Although time had laid its normal toll upon her body, her youthful spirit in Christ had not grown old. We stood at the gate of heaven and talked with one who had one foot inside the gate. In such a situation, we preferred to hear rather than be heard, to listen rather than to speak. So we listened to words "fitly spoken like apples of gold in pictures of silver."

This handmaiden of the Lord had a joyous testimony, even concerning her physical afflictions: "I had been going to a doctor for the past year or two to be treated for arthritis and the diseases incident to old age. About six months ago, I said to my doctor: 'You may not see me for a while. If I need you, I will either come to you or send for you.' I had promised God that if He would look after my body and take care of me physically, I would give to His cause what I had been paying the doctor. I had been paying the doctor about $5.00 per visit, one or two times a week. I promised God that I would give this money for His work. The Lord has watched over me and blessed me. He saved me from the winter diseases and He saved me from the spring diseases, and now we are starting into the summer and I am trusting the Lord to save me from the summer diseases. I am giving to the Lord's work all the money which I formerly gave to the doctor."

After engaging in such heavenly conversation for a time, our gracious hostess said: "I have had a custom for some years, when people come to see me of having a testimony meeting. I request my guests to speak concerning some events of the present day, for which they are thankful. I request them not to speak of events which transpired yesterday, or a week ago, or a month ago, but of some act of God's goodness and mercy related to their lives this present day. So in keeping with our custom, we shall now turn our conversation into a testimony meeting."

When she had spoken thus, she said to me: "What have you to be thankful for? What manifestations of God's grace have come to you today that you desire to speak of?"

I responded: "The thing that I have to be thankful for, more than anything that has happened today, is your witness and testimoney for your Lord and Saviour. I cannot begin to tell how much this has meant in the way of encouragement and the strengthening of my faith."

Mrs. McPheeters was then questioned in the same manner that I had been questioned: "What have you to be thankful for today?" Her testimony was similar to the one which I had given. Certainly the big thing of that particular day to us was the testimony of the woman who stood at the gate of heaven.

We listened with rapt attention as she spoke concerning the things that she had to be thankful for, things that had transpired on that very day. She said: "I have this to be thankful for today. The infirmities of age make it difficult for me to get downtown. But I went to town this morning and got back safely without harm or accident of any kind. I thank God for His protecting care that brought me safely home.

"There is another event that I want to thank God for. Early this morning, there came an old man to my door very much like an 'old bum' in his attire. He was soliciting the sharpening of scissors at seventy cents per pair. I said to him: 'You may sharpen my scissors and if you do a good job, I will give you one dollar.' The old man smoked and the smell of liquor was upon his breath. While he was sharpening my scissors, I prepared a nice sandwich lunch, put it in a sack and gave it to the old man. I prayed with him and gave my testimony concerning what Christ had meant in my life. I am so thankful that I had an opportunity to have a prayer with the old man and give my testimony and send him on his way with a bite to eat.

"There is still another matter in today's happenings that I want to thank God for. The laundryman came and I had the opportunity of witnessing to him as to what Christ has meant in my life. I rejoice so much in these opportunities which I have had to witness for my blessed Saviour."

Following these words of testimony, we knelt in prayer. Each one in the small circle offered a prayer of thanksgiving to God.

After the prayer, our good friend and spiritual benefactor gave a further word of testimony which was the crowning benediction of all the sacred things about which she had spoken. She said: "When I came to my 90th year, I promised God that I would do something special for Him, in recognition of His abiding mercy and grace, so bountifully manifest in my life. I told the Lord that it would be my purpose to do for Him during the year ninety different things that I had never done before. This means that I plan to do eight different things each month for six months, and then seven different things each month for six months. This way I hope to complete the quota of ninety different things I plan to do for the Lord in recognition of this my ninetieth year. I have made a good beginning and God has helped me thus far to carry out my plans. And now, I want to do something for you before you go."

She went to her desk and sat down to write a check. I surmised that this check might be in the amount of five or ten dollars. She rose from the desk with a smile and placed the check in my hand. I unfolded it and to my surprise it was written in the amount of $100. As I said, "Thank you," I could not restrain from saying, "Praise the Lord!" I said to her: "We are going to use this money for a scholarship in Asbury Theological Seminary for the coming school year. It is going to help some young man attend the seminary in preparation for the Christian ministry, who otherwise might not be able to attend."

What shall we say concerning such faith, such devotion, and such consecrated vision that ever abounds more and more in the Lord? In the light of this faith and devotion, are we not moved to pray the prayer which the disciples of Jesus prayed on one occasion: "Lord, increase our faith?" Surely we should be encouraged to press on in this "more excellent way," "from glory to glory," until we, too, shall stand at the very gate of heaven.

www.ingramcontent.com/pod-product-compliance
Lightning Source LLC
Chambersburg PA
CBHW020508040426
42331CB00042BA/86